Michelle Lovric is the creator of numerous bestselling anthologies and the author of the historical novel *Carnevale*. She lives in Venice and London.

Also by Michelle Lovric

Carnevale

The Virago Book of
christmas

Selected and Introduced
by

MICHELLE LOVRIC

Virago

contents

christmas abroad

the real gifts:
christmas transformations

christmas foods

mischief and malfeasance
at christmas

christmas at war

christmas romance

introduction

Christmas began with a good but harassed woman giving birth, with great joy, in difficult domestic circumstances.

Somewhere between then and now, circumstances have changed. We have moved on from stables and mangers to supermarkets and microwaves. The attendant iconography is no longer of palm fronds, shepherds and lambs, but of a fat, red-suited old man, a spangled conifer, an indigestion of ornament with a fake antiquarian patina, and an oversized sock stuffed with improbable items, some edible. The tyrannies are no longer of the tax collector, but of the gift list and the exigent rituals of the Christmas meal. For women today, however, Christmas is still a time of high pleasures garnered against stiff odds. In many ways, all women at Christmas have something in common with Mary: stress and happiness, in varying proportions.

This anthology, embracing letters, diaries, poems and stories, reflects the experiences at Christmas of more than fifty women from the fourteenth century to the present day.

Some women think back on Mary herself and that very first Christmas: the absence of womanly support at the nativity; the sheer impracticality of the gifts brought by the Three Kings. Others muse on the true meaning of the season, easily lost these days amid the obsessive toil to ensure its proper observances. Still others describe, with humour, the discomforts bravely weathered, the social tortures undergone.

Here, too, are writers who tell of disappointments faced with the grace of a Madonna, for Christmas raises in all of us breathless expectations that are almost impossible to fulfil. We are vulnerable, tender-skinned to any imperfection in the fabric of the day. Our demands are childlike. We want snow, or at least frost; we want the smell of wood-burning fires, the fragrant haze of holly; and voices – what the Germans call *Coterie-Sprache*, the language of intimates. We long for the perfect gift: Colette, for example, recalls her childhood desire for 'great scintillating tear-drops like those that hung beneath the chandeliers of a nearby château'. But if the gift can be a surprise, all the better.

Everyone deals with Christmas differently.

Certain women take a chary view. Emily Dickinson lists, in characteristically laconic style, her Christmas presents, observing that the candy in her stocking is unlikely to sweeten her nature. Adrian Mole, Sue Townsend's fictional teenage phenomenon, makes his own shopping list, just in case he finds ten pounds in the street. George Sand invites Flaubert for a family party, apologising in advance for the silliness of the season. Virginia Woolf and Edith Sitwell pen jaded Christmas letters, Sitwell in particular describing herself as 'a bad Christmasser'. Nothing, however, can match the misery of Jane Eyre's childhood, as recounted by Charlotte Brontë.

In other writers, especially those who chronicle life on the home front, Christmas brings out the warmth and the comedy. Stella Gibbons describes Christmas at Cold Comfort Farm, a squalid Starkadder Noel before the cleansing advent of Flora Poste. At the other end of the social scale, Lady Mary Wortley Montagu records with aplomb the unexpected arrival of thirty noble Italian ladies and gentlemen on horseback, all determined to celebrate Christmas with her, and Jane Carlyle describes Dickens seducing the crowds with his conjuring tricks at a classic Victorian party where William Thackeray and E.M. Forster were among the guests.

There are earthy childhood memories from Winifred Foley and more sophisticated recollections from Ntozake Shange and the actress Mrs Patrick Campbell. There are Christmas transformations from Elizabeth Goudge, and the surreal qualities of Christmases abroad evoked by Rose Macaulay, Valerie Josephs and Freya Stark.

Far from being the season of goodwill, Christmas can provoke the worst of crimes and misdemeanours. Agatha Christie's beloved sleuth puts the finger on its many provocations in an extract from *Hercule Poirot's Christmas*. Jenny Eclair, meanwhile, gives a comprehensive guide to festive bad behaviour. Other accounts of Christmas mischief and malfeasance come from Selma Lagerlöf and Nancy Mitford, while Cora Sandel and Clare Boylan provide some seasonal romance.

Christmas is particularly poignant during wartime when separations are inevitable and their misery intensified by nostalgia for happier times. The Tsarina Alexandra writes purring love letters to her adored Nicholas who is away at the Russian front. Rosa Luxemburg describes the Christmas of a political prisoner. Nobody who reads it is likely to forget the brutal climax to Vera Brittain's feverish preparations for her first

Christmas with her fiancé during World War I; and there's a short story of shiversome nuance from Elizabeth von Arnim, returning to Germany just before World War II. Edna Ferber records a cruel nativity in wartime Poland.

In better times, Christmas is, of course, a festival of greedy proportions. This anthology includes accounts of groaning tables by Rachel Ferguson and Coralie Bryant, while Spasenija Markovich, a little-known Serbian writer, describes the rituals of village hospitality between the wars in that long-suffering country.

In this book we have looked to present personal letters or lesser-known works by famous writers: material that has generally escaped the typical Christmas anthology. We have also sought to introduce some new, younger writers, whose views on Christmas reflect contemporary experience. In each case, though, the criterion for selection has been the same: to enrich and illuminate the festive season, whether by amusing, touching, or provoking the reader.

MICHELLE LOVRIC

the nativity:
mary's christmas

But what funny things to
give a baby – gold & myrrh
& frankincense. That's men
all over! It wouldn't cross
their minds to bring a shawl!

MOIRA ANDREW

Moira Andrew
(contemporary)

The Scots poet Moira Andrew has always enjoyed exploring with words and sounds, but only began writing professionally during the 1980s. She has two poetry collections for adults and many children's poems in publication. Most of her books are for primary school teachers, the best known of which is perhaps *Language in Colour*. Much of her work is based on her own teaching experience. Some of her poems reflect everyday happenings and childhood memories, others are purely imaginary. 'Letter from Egypt' was written in response to a request for a 'different kind of Christmas poem'. Moira Andrew now lives in Wales and works as a full-time writer and poet-in-schools.

Dear Miriam,
                    Just a line
to let you know how things
are with us & of course to
thank you (& your good man)
for all you did for us – &
at your busiest time too
what with the census &
everything. I was quite
exhausted & the baby was
beginning to make himself
felt. If it hadn't been
for your help that night
my baby might have died.

              Good of you
to put up with all our
visitors – who'd have
thought, six scruffy
shepherds up & leaving
their sheep like that?
& didn't they ever smell?
Still they were good-
hearted & they meant well.
I hope they brought some
extra trade to the inn.
They looked in need of
a hot drink & a meal.

            & what about
those Kings, Miriam? Kneeling
there in their rich robes
& all? & me in nothing but
my old blue dress! Joseph
said not to worry, it was
Jesus they'd come to see.
Real gentlemen *they* were.
But what funny things to
give a baby – gold & myrrh
& frankincense. That's men
all over! It wouldn't cross
their minds to bring a shawl!

           Sorry we left
so suddenly. No time for
good-byes with King Herod on
the warpath! We had to take
the long way home & I'm so
tired of looking at sand!
Joseph has picked up a few
jobs mending this & that so
we're managing quite well.
Jesus grows bonnier every
day & thrives on this way
of life, but I can't wait
to see Nazareth again.

               Love to all
               at the inn,
                  Mary

Saint Bridget of Sweden
(1303–73)

Saint Bridget, the patron saint of Sweden, was born into a noble family in Finsta in Uppland. She was subject to mystical visions from an early age. Married at 13, she persuaded her husband to remain chaste for two years but eventually bore him eight children. The couple went on a pilgrimage to Santiago de Compostela in 1341. When her husband died two years later, Bridget withdrew to her own spiritual world and founded a new order of nuns. She dictated her spiritual revelations and moved to Rome, where she stayed for the rest of her life, apart from making a pilgrimage to the Holy Land in 1372. In this passage from *Revelations*, she describes the nativity in warm and intimate detail.

'When I was present by the manager of the Lord in Bethlehem, I beheld a Virgin of extreme beauty well wrapped in a white mantle and a delicate tunic through which I clearly perceived her virgin body. With her was an old man of great honesty, and they brought with them an ox and ass. These entered the cave, and the man after having tied them to the manger went outside and brought to the Virgin a burning candle, and having attached this to the wall, he went outside again so that he might not be present at the birth. Then the Virgin pulled off the shoes from her feet, drew off the white mantle that enveloped her, removed the veil from her head, laying it by her side, thus remaining in her tunic alone, with her beautiful golden hair falling loosely over her shoulders. Then she produced two small linen cloths and two woollen ones of exquisite purity and fineness which she had brought to wrap up the Child who was to be born, and two other small pieces with which to cover and bind His Head, and these she then sat down on the ground, laying the Child on her lap, and at once she began to bestow on Him much care, tying up His small body, His legs and arms with long cloths. Then she enveloped the head of the Child in two linen garments prepared for the purpose, and when this was done the old man entered, and prostrating himself on the floor he wept for joy. And in no way was the Virgin changed by birth, neither as to the colour of her face nor as to any illness, and her bodily strength did not decline, as is usually the case with women when they bear. But then she stood up, and together the two, that is herself and Joseph, put Him in the manager and on their knees worshipped Him with immense joy until the arrival of the Kings, and the Kings recognised the Son from His likeness to His Mother.'

Emily (Emma) Henrietta Hickey
(1845–1924)

The largely forgotten Victorian poet Emma Hickey was born in Ireland but spent most of her life in England. She supported herself by working as a governess and a secretary and by contributing articles to magazines. From 1878 until 1894 she lectured in English literature at the North London Collegiate School for Girls. Influenced by William Morris, Algernon Swinburne and Robert Browning, Hickey wrote religious poems and verse based on Irish legends. Her love poems usually deal with impossible unions; she herself never married. After her conversion to Roman Catholicism in 1901, her poetry concerned itself more with the state of the soul than with human love. Several volumes of her poetry were published during her lifetime and the collection, *Christmas Verse*, appeared posthumously. 'The First Christmas Eve' was published by the Catholic Truth Society in 1902.

There was no room within the inn for them:
The Woman that beneath her girdle bare
The Hope of all the world, a stranger there
Lay, all that solemn night, in Bethlehem
Within a stable; Jesse's root and stem
Should spring the very morrow strong and fair,
And all the slumbering world was unaware.
We, who still slumber, how shall we condemn?

She lies, all one with God, this holy eve;
She, whose glad eyes will look to-morrow morn
With rapture on the blessed Man-child born;
She, who in three-and-thirty years will grieve,
Pierced to the heart; she, who will yet receive
The garland of the rose without a thorn.

II

Oh, was there never a woman there to say,
Behold, this woman nears her travailing
And take her by the hand and gently bring
Into a room, and softly speak, and lay
The woman down, and watch by her till day,
When shade should flee and from on high should
    spring
The Light of Light, for help and comforting?
We, blind and cold, nor dare to blame, nor may.

And yet, if men had felt the throbbing breast
Of night alive with wonder and the fair
Great dawn, they had left their beds all empty there,
Nor cared one whit for any sleep or rest.
We, have not we rejected any guest?
Dismissed the more than angel unaware?

Edna Ferber
(1887–1968)

The distinguished American writer Edna Ferber was born in Kalamazoo, Michigan, the daughter of a shopkeeper. When her father became blind, she had to work to support the family, and became a journalist. Ferber was the author of numerous novels and short stories, including *So Big* (1924), for which she won the Pulitzer Prize. She famously collaborated with George Kaufman in a number of plays, including *Dinner at Eight* (1932) and *Stage Door* (1936). Ferber is probably best remembered as the author of *Show Boat* (1926) on which the eponymous musical is based, and for *Giant* (1952), which was made into a film starring James Dean, the last film he made before he died. Her writings reveal her great interest in the American middle class and she has been described as a 'chronicler of American cultural history'.

This story, 'No Room at the Inn', describes a different kind of nativity – one far more brutal than the traditional Christmas story.

Here is pure plagiarism. My source is the Eternal Best Seller. I happened to read in The New York Times *the brief and poignant news paragraph quoted at the top of this story. The persecution, torture, and death of six million European Jews had actually brought little or no protest from a Christian world whose religion was based on the teachings of a Jew.*

I took the story and characters involved in the birth of the infant Jesus and modernized these to fit the German Nazi pattern. So Joe, Mary, Lisabeth, and Zach are rather well known to you – I hope. It is to be regretted that this story, written in 1939, is not what we call dated even today in 1946.

'NOBODY' IS BORN IN NO MAN'S LAND

Prague, Oct. 25 (U.P.) – *A baby born in the no man's land south of Brno, where 200 Jewish refugees have been living in a ditch between Germany and Czechoslovakia for two weeks, was named Niemand (Nobody) today.*

She had made every stitch herself. Literally, every stitch, and the sewing was so fairylike that the eye scarcely could see it. Everything was new, too. She had been almost unreasonable about that, considering Joe's meager and uncertain wage and the frightening time that had come upon the world. Cousin Elisabeth had offered to give her some of the clothing that her baby had outgrown, but Mary had refused, politely, to accept these.

'That is dear and good of you, 'Lisbeth,' Mary had said. 'I know it seems ungrateful, maybe, and even silly not to take them. It's hard to tell you how I feel. I want everything of his to be new. I want to make everything myself. Every little bit myself.'

Cousin Elisabeth was more than twice as old as Mary. She understood everything. It was a great comfort to have Elisabeth so near, with her wisdom and her warm sympathy. 'No, I don't think it's silly at all. I know just how you feel. I felt the same way when my John was coming.' She laughed then, teasingly: 'How does it happen you're so sure it's going to be a boy? You keep saying "he" all the time.'

Mary had gone calmly on with her sewing, one infinitesimal stitch after the other, her face serene. 'I know. I know.' She glanced up at her older cousin, fondly. 'I only hope he'll be half as smart and good as your little John.'

Elisabeth's eyes went to the crib where the infant lay asleep. 'Well, if I say so myself, John certainly is smart for his age. But then' – hastily, for fear that she should seem too proud – 'but, then, Zach and I are both kind of middle-aged. And they say the first child of middle-aged parents is likely to be unusually smart.'

The eighteen-year-old Mary beamed at this. 'Joe's middle-aged!' she boasted happily. Then she blushed the deep, flaming crimson of youth and innocence; for Joe's astonishment at the first news of the child's coming had been as great as her own. It was like a miracle wrought by some outside force.

Cousin Elisabeth had really made the match between the young girl and the man well on in years. People had thought it strange; but this Mary, for all her youth, had a wisdom and sedateness beyond her years, and an unexpected humor, too,

quiet and strangely dry, such as one usually finds associated
with long observation and experience. Joe was husband, father,
brother to the girl. It was wonderful. They were well mated.
And now, when life in this strange world had become so frightening, so brutal, so terrible, it was more than ever wonderful to
have his strength and goodness and judgment as a shield and
staff. She knew of younger men, hotheaded, who had been
taken away in the night and never again heard from. Joe went
quietly about his business. But each morning as he left her he
said, 'Stay at home until I come back this evening. Or, if you
must do your marketing, take Elisabeth with you. I'll stop by
and tell her to call for you. Don't go into the streets alone.'

'I'll be all right,' she said. 'Nobody would hurt me.' For here
pregnant women were given special attention. The government
wanted children for future armies.

'Not our children,' Joe said bitterly.

So they lived quietly, quietly they obeyed the laws; they went
nowhere. Two lower-middle-class people. Dreadful, unspeakable things were happening; but such things did not happen to
her and to her husband and to her unborn child. Everything
would right itself. It must.

Her days were full. There were two rooms to keep clean, the
marketing, the cooking, the sewing. The marketing was a tiring
task, for one had to run from shop to shop to get a bit of butter,
an egg for Joe, a piece of meat however coarse and tough.
Sometimes when she came back to the little flat in the narrow
street and climbed the three flights of stairs, the beads of sweat
stood on her lip and forehead and her breath came painfully, for
all her youth. Still, it was glorious to be able at night to show

Joe a pan of coffeecake or a meatball, or even a pat of pretty good butter. On Friday she always tried her hardest to get a fowl, however skinny, or a bit of beef or lamb because Friday was the eve of the Sabbath. She rarely could manage it, but that made all the sweeter her triumph when she did come home, panting up the stairs, with her scrap of booty.

Mary kept her sewing in a wicker basket neatly covered over with a clean white cloth. The little pile grew and grew. Joe did not know that she had regularly gone without a midday meal in order to save even that penny or two for the boy's furnishings. Sometimes Joe would take the sewing from her busy hands and hold it up, an absurd fragment of cloth, a miniature garment that looked the smaller in contrast with his great, work-worn hand. He would laugh as he held it, dangling. It seemed so improbable that anything alive and sentient should be small enough to fit into this scrap of cloth. Then, in the midst of his laugh, he would grow serious. He would stare at her and she at him and they would listen, hushed, as for a dreaded and expected sound on the stairs.

Floors to scrub, pots and pans to scour, clothes to wash, food to cook, garments to sew. It was her life, it was for Joe, it was enough and brimming over. Hers was an enormous pride in keeping things in order, the pride of possession inherited from peasant ancestors. Self-respect.

The men swarmed up the stairway so swiftly that Mary and Joe had scarcely heard their heavy boots on the first landing before they were kicking at the door and banging it with their fists. Joe sprang to his feet and she stood up, one hand at her breast and in that hand a pink knitted hood, no bigger than a fist, that she was knitting. Then they were in the room; they filled the little clean room with their clamor and their oaths and their great brown-clad bodies. They hardly looked at Joe and Mary, they ransacked the cupboards, they pulled out the linen and the dishes, they trampled these. One of the men snatched the pink cap from her hand and held it up and then put it on his own big, round head, capering with a finger in his mouth.

'Stop that!' said one in charge. 'We've no time for such foolishness.' And snatched off the pink hood, and blew his nose into it, and threw it in a corner.

In the cupboard they came upon the little cakes. She had saved drippings, she had skimmed such bits of rare fat as came their way, she had used these to fashion shortening for four little cakes, each with a dab of dried plum on top. Joe had eaten two for his supper and there had been two left for his breakfast. She had said she did not want any. Cakes made her too fat. It was bad for the boy.

'Look!' yelled the man who had found these. 'Cakes! These swine have cakes to eat, so many that they can leave them uneaten in the cakebox.' He broke one between his fingers, sniffed it like a dog, then bolted it greedily.

'Enough of this!' yelled the man in authority. 'Stop fooling and come on! You want to stay in this pigsty all night! There's a hundred more. Come on. Out!'

Then they saw Mary, big as she was, and they made a joke of this, and one of them poked her a little with his finger, and still Joe did nothing, he was like a man standing asleep with his eyes wide open. Then they shoved them both from the room.

As they went, Mary made a gesture toward the basket in the corner – the basket that had been covered so neatly with the clean white cloth. Her hand was outstretched; her eyes were terrible. The little stitches so small that even she had scarcely been able to see them, once she had pricked them into the cloth.

The man who had stuffed the cakes into his mouth was now hurriedly wiping his soiled boots with a bit of soft white, kneeling by the overturned basket as he did so. He was very industrious and concentrated about it, as they were taught to be thorough about everything. His tongue was out a little way between his strong yellow teeth and he rubbed away industriously. Then, at an impatient oath from the leader, he threw the piece of cloth into a corner with the rest of the muddied, trampled garments and hurried after so that he was there to help load them into the truck with the others huddled close.

Out of the truck and on the train they bumped along for hours – or it may have been days. Mary had no sense of time. Joe pillowed her head on his breast and she even slept a little, like a drugged thing, her long lashes meeting the black smudges under her eyes. There was no proper space for them all; they huddled on the floor and in the passages. Soon the scene was one of indescribable filth. Children cried, some-times women screamed hysterically, oftenest they sat, men and women, staring into space. The train puffed briskly along with the businesslike efficiency characteristic of the country.

It was interesting to see these decent middle-class people

reduced to dreadful squalor, to a sordidness unthought of in their lives. From time to time the women tried to straighten their clothing, to wash their bodies, but the cup of water here and there was needed for refreshment. Amidst these stenches and sounds, amidst the horror and degradation, Joe and Mary sat, part of the scene, yet apart from it. She had wakened curiously refreshed. It was as though a dream she had dreamed again and again, only to awake in horror, had really come to pass, and so, seeing it come true, she was better able to bear it, knowing the worst of it. Awake, she now laid his head in its turn on her breast and through exhaustion he slept, his eyes closed flutteringly but his face and hands clenched even in sleep. Joe had aged before her eyes, overnight. A strong and robust man, of sturdy frame, he had withered; there were queer hollows in his temples and blue veins throbbed there in welts she had never before seen.

Big though she was with her burden, she tried to help women younger and older than she. She was, in fact, strangely full of strength and energy, as often is the case with pregnant women.

The train stopped, and they looked out, and there was nothing. It started again, and they came to the border of the next country. Men in uniform swarmed amongst them, stepping over them and even on them as if they were vermin. Then they talked together and alighted from the train, and the train backed until it came again to the open fields where there was nothing. Barren land, and no sign of habitation. It was nowhere. It was nothing. It was neither their country nor the adjoining country. It was no man's land.

They could not enter here, they could not turn back there. Out they went, shoved and pushed, between heaven and hell, into purgatory. Lost souls.

They stumbled out into the twilight. It was October, it was today. Nonsense, such things do not happen, this is a civilized world, they told themselves. Not like this, to wander until they dropped and died.

They walked forward together, the two hundred of them, dazedly but with absurd purposefulness, too, as if they were going somewhere. The children stumbled and cried and stumbled again. Shed, barn, shelter there was none. There was nothing.

And then that which Mary had expected began to take place. Her pains began, wave on wave. Her eyes grew enormous and her face grew very little and thin and old. Presently she could no longer walk with the rest. They came upon a little flock of sheep grazing in a spot left still green in the autumn, and near by were two shepherds and a tiny donkey hardly bigger than a dog.

Joe went to the shepherds, desperate. 'My wife is ill. She is terribly ill. Let me take your donkey. There must be some place near by – an inn. Some place.'

One of the shepherds, less oafish than the other, and older, said, 'There's an inn, but they won't take her.'

'Here,' said Joe, and held out a few poor coins that had been in his pocket. 'Let her ride just a little way.'

The fellow took the coins. 'All right. A little way. I'm going home. It's suppertime. She can ride a little way.'

So they hoisted her to the donkey's back and she crouched

there, but presently it was her time, and she slipped off and they helped her to the ditch by the side of the road.

She was a little silly by now, what with agony and horror. 'Get all the nice clean things, Joe. The linen things, they're in the box in the cupboard. And call Elisabeth. Put the kettle on to boil. No, not my best nightgown, that comes later, when everything is over and I am tidy again. Men don't know.'

Her earth rocked and roared and faces were blurred and distorted and she was rent and tortured and she heard someone making strange noises like an animal in pain, and then there came merciful blackness.

When she awoke there were women bending over her, and they had built a fire from bits of wood and dried grass, and in some miraculous way there was warm water and strips of cloth and she felt and then saw the child by her side in the ditch and he was swaddled in decent wrappings. She was beyond the effort of questioning, but at the look in her eyes the woman bending over her said, 'It's a boy. A fine boy.' And she held him up. He waved his tiny arms and his hair was bright in the reflection of the fire behind him. But they crowded too close around her, and Joseph waved them away with one arm and slipped his other under her head and she looked up at him and even managed to smile.

As the crowd parted there was the sound of an automobile that came to a grinding halt. They were officials, you could see that easily enough, with their uniforms and their boots and their proud way of walking.

'Hr-r-rmph!' they said. 'Here, all of you. Now then, what's all this! We had a hell of a time finding you, we never would have got here if we hadn't seen the light in the sky from your fire. Now, then, answer to roll call; we've got the names of all of you, so speak up or you'll wish you had.'

They called the roll of the two hundred and each answered, some timidly, some scornfully, some weeping, some cringing, some courageously.

'Mary!' they called. 'Mary.'

She opened her eyes. 'Mary,' she said, in little more than a whisper.

'That must be the one,' they said amongst themselves, the three. 'That's the one had the kid just born.' They came forward then and saw the woman Mary and the newborn babe in the ditch. 'Yep, that's it. Born in a ditch to one of these damned Jews.'

'Well, let's put it on the roll call. Might as well get it in now, before it grows up and tries to sneak out. What d'you call it! Heh, Mary?' He prodded her a little, not too roughly, with the toe of his boot.

She opened her eyes again and smiled a little as she looked up at him and then at the boy in her arm. She smiled while her eyes were clouded with agony.

'Niemand,' she whispered.

'What's that? Speak up! Can't hear you.'

She concentrated all her energies, she formed her lips to make sound again, and licked them because they were quite dry, and said once more, 'Niemand . . . Nobody.'

One man wrote it down, but the first man stared as though he resented being joked with, a man of his position. But at the look in her eyes he decided that she had not been joking. He stared and stared at the boy, the firelight shining on his tiny face, making a sort of halo of his hair.

'Niemand, eh? That the best you can do for him! . . . Jesus! . . . Well, cheer up, he's a fine-looking boy. He might grow up to be quite a kid, at that.'

U. A. Fanthorpe
(1929–)

Ursula Askham Fanthorpe was born in London and studied at St Anne's College, Oxford and the University of London Institute of Education before teaching English at Cheltenham Ladies' College. She also spent several years working as a hospital clerk and drew on these experiences when writing her wry, often darkly humorous poems. In 2001 Fanthorpe was awarded an OBE for services to literature and was the first woman ever to be nominated for the post of Oxford Professor of Poetry. She was championed by the *Guardian* newspaper as a candidate for Poet Laureate when Ted Hughes died. Her volumes of poetry include *Voices Off* (1984) and *Consequences* (2000). She has said, 'I'm interested in neglected places, and in the boundaries of language, the language of small children, the inarticulate and the mentally confused. The thing I hate is power. I'm sorry for the people who have it because of the things it does to them.' Two Christmas poems are included here, 'Angels' Song' and 'The Contributors'.

Intimates of heaven,
This is strange to us,
The unangelic muddle,
The birth, the human fuss.

We sing a harder carol now:
Holy the donkey in the hay;
Holy the manger made of wood,
Holy the nails, the blood, the clay.

Not your fault, gentlemen.
We acquit you of the calculatedly
Equivalent gift, the tinsel token.
Mary, maybe, fancied something more practical:
A layette, or at least a premium bond.
Firmly you gave the extravagantly
Useless, your present the unwrapped
Hard-edged stigma of vocation.

Not your fault, beasts,
Who donated your helpless animal
Rectitude to the occasion.
Not yours the message of the goblin
Robin, the red-nosed reindeer,
Nor had you in mind the yearly
Massacre of the poultry innocent,
Whom we judge correct for the feast.

Not your fault, Virgin,
Muddling along in the manger,
With your confused old man,
Your bastard baby, in conditions
No social worker could possibly approve.
How could your improvised, improvident
Holiness predict our unholy family Xmas,
Our lonely overdoses, deepfrozen bonhomie?

childhood christmases

At the bottom of my piece of the bed was propped the ugliest apology for a doll one could ever hope not to see.

WINIFRED FOLEY

Coralie Bryant
(1942–)

Coralie Bryant is of Norwegian ancestry, and grew up in a Scandinavian community in northern Minnesota. With degrees in music and literature, she has worked as an educator in both her native United States and in Canada, including several years in the Northwest Territories. She worked with Michael Hayhoe and Patrick Dias on the International Poetry Project and contributed to Developing Response to Poetry (Open University Press) at its conclusion. Recently retired from a school superintendency, she serves as Vice-Chair of the Manitoba Arts Council and does some consulting.

Her poem 'Returning' describes the mixing of Scandinavian and Canadian customs in a magical childhood Christmas.

Christmas in Roseau (that prairie town)
many years ago
when we were kids
we remember
sometimes imperfectly
in detail
but perfectly
in emotion
surely
for how could a thing
so perfect, so powerful
live otherwise
in our hearts?
It was our mother's doing,
She
and the church . . .

The heavy carved wood panelling,
higharched stained windows
and long oak pews
made the church
cozy at Christmas
with white candles blazing
and the air heavy with the
incense of fresh cedar boughs
and Norway pine.
One tall tree freshly cut
and hauled from the woods
stood as high as the

cathedral ceiling,
presiding over solemn rituals,
the tallest Christmas tree
we had ever seen
(this was much before the town
began to erect its own
on the river bank
near where the
church then
stood).

A holiness
next to Christmas itself
was the Sunday
of the choir concerts;
Christmas really began then.
The big ones, including Dad,
sang with the senior choir,
the little ones in sweet and true
two and three-part harmony;
twice – at four o'clock and eight –
the candlelit church
filled to capacity
with faces from all over town
faces strange to our church
except at Christmas.
It was wondrous,
those new crinkly Christmas clothes
under white or green choir gowns;

the college kids – so much older
than a few months ago,
their voices strong, fuller now
in the prized solos and quartettes,
guests of honor,
for they bestowed a dignity
to the occasion we could never
have managed alone.
But always Carl Dahlquist
sand *Jeg Jer Saa Glad*,
Don Norlin sent shivers down the spine
singing *O Holy Night*,
and whoever was the current
lucky loveliest mezzo soprano
made Christmas come
with *Lullaby on Christmas Eve*.

Mother didn't sing.
That is hard to believe now,
this woman in her seventies
who sings everywhere,
in trios and quartettes,
in costume and out,
both sacred and silly stuff,
astonishing
her children, but not the people
who have lived by her
for fifty years. She stayed home
then: some of us

were too young to sing,
or there was too much to do,
or one of us was sick.
One year we arrived home
to see a fireplace
against the wall
made ingeniously
from cardboard and red paper.
Stockings were hung.
We had never before had stockings.
Our hearts nearly stopped
for joy.

When I was older
my father would ask me
sometimes
on the morning of Christmas Eve
what I thought Mother would like
for Christmas.
The importance I felt
in being consulted
outweighed my outrage
on her behalf.
That he loved her
I knew.
But of all days of the year
in our home
this is the only one
I clearly remember

smell taste and hear
still. December 24th.
A day it seemed then
made not so much by God
as by
our mother.

We had lists
in the morning, those
little white squares with
three or four chores written down,
a neat box before each
so we could check them off
as we finished.
The rules were never discussed,
only handed down
from child to child:
'the lists stay on the table
so Mother can check them
from time to time';
'no one plays till the
work's done'.
This Saturday routine applied also
on December 24th
until the whole house
shone.

We would all bundle up warmly
at four o'clock
to go caroling around the town

with the Junior Choir.
In cars or on foot, we'd go
from house to house
singing to invalids and
the old
in stale porches, or
sometimes invited
with our snowy boots
still on
into overheated living rooms,
sour-smelling and sad,
lit up by three lights
and the beatific smiles
of the old gazing upon the young.

Poverty, illness and the lonely were
quickly forgotten as we stripped off
sodden scarves, mitts and boots, and
raced to change for Christmas supper.
The house smelled of lutefisk
and mashed potatoes and melted butter
and of flatbread and sweetpotatoes
and Swedish potato sausage (for the
only non-Norwegian at table,
Uncle Carl) and of pies and cookies,
of ginger, nutmeg, and brown sugar,
and of the tree, brought from the woods.
The table was already laid for nine,
and our cousins might already be

there, emptying boxes of gifts
carried in from the car
and putting them under the tree.
(When we were small,
Dad set the tree
into a playpen
to keep the younger kids
from tampering
with the gifts.)

Once a solemn grace was said,
we ate till we could not
stuff in one more bit of
lefse, spread and rolled
with butter and brown sugar
nor could we have stood
another minute of anticipation.
Time stood breathlessly
mercilessly
still
while the mothers
did the dishes,
the fathers talked
and smoked cigars
and we kids
prepared a program
to begin the evening –
another excuse, we thought,
to prolong our agony.

At last,
everyone sitting round,
we sang, and read Luke 2
and otherwise solemnly
summoned Christmas
as briefly as
we thought
we could get by with.
Finally, the moment:
the tension over which
child would be Santa
and deliver all the gifts,
the interminable
wait till it was our turn
to receive one,
tear it open,
wonder briefly about parents
how *they* felt
opening their
presents
(could it possibly feel the same?)

When it was all over,
(how could that be? there
had been thousands of gifts!)
dessert and coffee and
platters of Christmas cookies and candy,
krumkaka, rosettes and sandbakkelse
would appear. How could

they interest anyone, we wondered,
as we reveled in our new things,
longing already for
Christmas morning,
when the real Santa
would bring something more,
something special –
once, even a phonograph
for the whole family.

Christmas Day brought Yulekaka,
church and skating
all afternoon,
hours to spend
at the rink
pushing our limbs to the limit,
then walking home in the biting
twilight air, exhausted, content,
and a little disappointed.
Only our parents, now
would disguise themselves in
silly costumes and
go Yulebakking
through the town,
singing and
fooling their friends, and then
plan New Year's card parties
where we might have a sip of
Mother's homemade berry wine

if we were clever.
For us it was really all over,
December 25,
somewhere around five
in the afternoon.

Returning to the town where
we used to live –
the house and church
are gone
and so is Dad
but Mother is there
still making lefse
that melts in our mouths
and lutefisk that
makes us hunger
for our norske beginnings.
The house is hung with lights
and everywhere made gay for
her children's
and grandchildren's
glad homecoming.
And, going there, we now sing
altogether, round the tree,
as we did long ago.

The happy Christmas comes once more,
The heavenly guest is at the door.
The blessed words the shepherds thrill
The joyous tidings, 'Peace, goodwill'.

Winifred Foley
(1914–)

Winifred Foley was born, the daughter of a miner, in the small village of Brierley, in Gloucestershire's Forest of Dean. She grew up in a close-knit community and a loving family where poverty and hunger were no strangers. At fourteen she left her rural home to find work 'in service' in London and in the Cotswolds. It was not, however, until she was 60 that she demonstrated a rare gift for dialogue and vivid recall, when she wrote her now celebrated *A Child in the Forest*, chronicling her working class upbringing during the early part of the twentieth century. Her story was read in serial form on BBC *Woman's Hour*, immediately became a national bestseller, and was the inspiration for several television dramas and a stage play, as well as further serialisations on radio. The sequel to *A Child in the Forest*, entitled *No Pipe Dreams for Father*, tells the story of Foley's teenage years. The concluding volume, *Back to the Forest*, is the story of her return to live in her beloved Forest of Dean with a family of her own after World War II.

This extract comes from *A Child in the Forest*, first published in 1974. Foley's child character, a strong personality with a rich and comical turn of phrase, refuses to be placated either by adult explanations or with an unsatisfactory gift – until she is provoked to display an uncompromising loyalty of her own.

If the chapel treat was the highlight of our life in summer, Christmas was the pinnacle of our winter delight, though most of the joy was in the anticipation. Every year for many years I spent weeks getting excited about a hopeless dream. I wanted – oh how I wanted – a doll. I knew it was quite impossible for Mam and Dad to buy me one. I had no luck praying for one, and it wasn't any good asking Dad to put a word in for me in that quarter, because I'd heard him and his butties argue and come to the conclusion that there couldn't be a God, or at any rate not one who worried about us as individuals.

But Father Christmas was quite a likely benefactor, though he too had his limitations. My dad had explained to me that as Father Christmas was such an old man, with his long white beard, he couldn't be expected to carry big things for all the children. I should have to wait my turn for a doll. Meantime I must be satisfied with something small, like a penny box of beads, and an orange if I was lucky. My turn for a doll seemed a long time coming.

My patience ran out one autumn when I was nine years old. Gladys, my best friend, who already had a nice doll, was given the most fantastic doll you ever saw. I didn't begrudge Gladys anything – she let me nurse her doll, and dress and undress it. But that was like being a nanny, not the same as having your own baby. The new doll was the size of a child, had long hair, eyes that opened and shut, and wore socks and shoes. Gladys's dad had won it at Barton fair. The doll was much too grand to play with, and was put on display in their cottage. All the village children, and quite a few grown-ups, called at Gladys's home for the privilege of seeing it.

As far as I was concerned, matters regarding a doll had now come to a head. I couldn't help Father Christmas's decrepitude – he would *have* to bring me a doll this Christmas. I gave him plenty of warning by shouting my request up the chimney weeks in advance of the usual time. Towards Christmas I started to write notes to him as well, with a stub of pencil given me by a neighbour as payment for running errands.

I was puzzling out how best to put my case to him with the limited spelling and vocabulary of a nine-year-old, when Dad came in. I told him I was making a bargain with Father Christmas: providing he brought me a doll this time, he needn't bring me anything else ever. But it had to be a doll big enough to sit on my lap, and have hair, and eyes that opened and shut.

'I be a-feared 'tis no good thee exing Feyther Christmas for that sart o' doll, my wench. 'Im do only take that sart to the rich people's young uns,' Dad warned me kindly.

'You do want to tell the silly old bugger off then. Tell 'im they rich people can afford to buy dolls for their children. It's the likes o' we lot 'im do want to bring the best toys to. Why ever 'aven't 'im got more sense then that?'

Father, who usually had an explanation for everything under the sun, scratched his head and admitted himself 'proper flummoxed'.

Bess said I'd be lucky to get anything if Father Christmas overheard me calling him a silly old bugger. Just because she was gone thirteen years old, and would soon be going into domestic service, she fancied herself too grown-up to ask Father Christmas for anything. Anyway, then she would be rich enough to buy anything she wanted, for my auntie in Bristol was getting her a job with the fantastic wage of five shillings a week.

With hope only slightly diminished, I continued to shout my order up the chimney, and to send up my notes when the draught was strong enough to stop them falling back into the fire.

My little brother fell asleep on Christmas Eve long before I did. I kept poking him awake to keep me company, but it was no good. I must have been awake for hours, when I heard stealthy footsteps coming up the stairs. It must be Father Christmas! Should I look, or shouldn't I? I had the patchwork quilt pulled right up to my eyes – he wouldn't notice, if I just took a peep. I suddenly felt terrified.

It was a bit of an anticlimax when I saw my sister in the doorway! 'Oh gawd! I thought you was Feyther Christmas!' It seemed to me that she was hiding something behind her back.

'If thee doosn't go to sleep Feyther Christmas wunt come at all,' she scolded me.

'I can't,' I wailed, 'thee'lt 'a' to 'it I over the yud wi' the coal 'ammer.'

I banged my obstinate head into the bolster. 'Go to sleep, you silly little bitch,' I told myself crossly.

It was my excited little brother who poked *me* awake in the morning. 'Look – Feyther Christmas a' brought I a tin whistle, a orange, a bag o' marbles an' some sweets.'

I sat bolt upright, like a Jack-in-the-Box. My doll, my doll! Had Father Christmas brought my doll?

At the bottom of my piece of the bed was propped the ugliest apology for a doll one could ever hope not to see.

It looked for all the world like an old, darned, black woollen stocking, lumpily stuffed, with a bit of old ribbon tied tightly round the foot to form its head. The eyes were two odd-sized buttons, and it grimaced from ear to ear with a red woollen gash of a mouth.

After all that cajoling up the chimney, after all the notes I'd written, fancy him bringing me a thing like that! He must think me a horrible little girl to treat me so, but I couldn't be that horrible! Mam came in, looking a bit anxious, but she said, bright enough, 'Well, then, Feyther Christmas didn't forget. 'Im did bring a doll for you.'

'Yes, an' 'im can 'ave the bugger back.'

Mother looked crestfallen. 'It won't break, like one o' they china dolls.'

'It's ugly, an' boss-eyed, an' got no 'air, and 'ow would you like it if the angels sent you a baby as ugly as *that*?'

Then I pulled the quilt over my head, to show I had cut myself off from the season of goodwill, and everyone concerned with it.

But Mam hadn't. After a bit she came back and sat on the bed. She didn't say anything, and my curiosity soon overcame me enough to have a peep at what she was up to.

Her baby boy, born a year after my little brother, had died; I thought he'd gone to heaven to be pampered and fussed over by the angels. Mam had kept a few of his baby clothes, though in general the women in our part of the village pooled their baby clothes to help each other out. Now she was dressing my doll up in a flannel nightdress, a bonnet and a piece of shawl. Held up in Mam's arms and cuddled against her neck, it looked like a real infant from the back. I was tempted to be won round. Mam left it, all snugly wrapped up, on the bed, while she went to get breakfast.

I and the doll were soon downstairs with the rest of the family, sitting at the table. Mam was in a specially good humour with me. We didn't have such things as bacon and eggs even on Christmas Day, but as a great treat old Auntie had given us half a tin of Nestlé's milk to share out on our toast. As if that were not enough, she'd given us each a shiny new penny as well. I felt warmed and loved again. I made a bit of sop in a saucer, with a drop of my tea and a bit of the bread and milk, and pretended to spoon it into my doll's mouth, before taking her out.

I knew that other children might laugh at her ugliness as they did at Lil Wills's poor little looney sister, so I decided to take her for a walk on my own. Miss Phillips, whose cottage garden adjoined ours, was just coming back from the ashmix with an empty bucket.

'My, my, Polly! It looks as though Feyther Christmas 'a' brought you a real big doll this time. Let me 'ave a look at 'er.'

I loved the inside of Miss Phillips' neat, tidy cottage, but none of us were much taken with her – she nagged us for playing nosily, and wouldn't let us play ball where we wanted to. I gave her one of my ferocious scowls to put her off, but she insisted on following me and unwrapping the piece of shawl to see what I'd got.

'Oh my gawd, that'un 'ould do better to frighten the birds off the gyarden. I reckon Feyther Christmas musta took 'im from a crow's nest.'

How dare she! I bridled like an insulted mother! I doubled my scowl, and threw in my monkey face for good measure.

'Never mind,' I said to the doll, when we were out of earshot. 'Er's a nasty old bisom, and your mammy 'ouldn't change you for all the money in the world.'

Miss Phillips' insults cemented my feeling for my new charge. From then, she became the object of my affection.

Sidonie-Gabrielle Colette
(1873–1954)

Colette was born in a small village in Burgundy. Her childhood was reasonably happy, although she had to leave school at sixteen when her father's mismanagement cost the family its fortune. However, she continued to be an enthusiastic reader and she began to write the *Claudine* novels under the tutelage of her first husband, Henri Gauthier-Villars, who was a talented editor. They were published under his pen-name 'Willy'. After their divorce in 1906, she appeared in music-halls in dance and mime for a time. She continued to write; her novels, including *Chérie, La Vagabonde* and *Gigi*, were immensely popular. Colette's intense, sensual but cynical nature is evident both in her novels and in the numerous letters she wrote to her friends and family. She married Henri de Jouvenel in 1912 and Maurice Goudeket in 1935. She was elected to the Académie Goncourt in 1945 and given the Grand Cross of the Légion d'Honneur in 1953. Colette was the first woman in France to be accorded a state funeral.

This evocative passage comes from her book *De ma Fenêtre*, first published in 1942, and muses on French childhood Christmases, both town and country. Colette looks dreamily back and forwards in time, comparing and drawing together her experiences as a child and as the mother of a child.

*

Midnight Mass at five in the afternoon . . . Children, you won't
have had your young vigil in the expectation of a luminous
midnight. You won't have had the departure and return with
lanterns. You will have been satisfied with the night in the
church, burning bushes, flowers dedicated to Jesus, evergreens
which mingle with the incense the aromas of box, laurel and
fir. It sufficed to enchant your sensibility, which is responsive to
every stimulus. What you have had will ensure that your memories, later on, will tell you of Parisian midnight that sounded
five strokes.

Paris is too dark for you to be allowed to stumble about in it,
you children who, for one night in the year, haunt the streets
and go to bed late. I loved meeting you during this past year
under the lights – already dimmed – at the moment when you
were returning from a mass, a fête held under the branches of
a tree. You were the luminous signposts on my journey for, in
passing, you threw me the glitter of some spangled toy – a
walnut, a branch of grapes, an apple of spun and gilded glass,
a tinfoil crown – children, our future, our last treasure . . .

Christmas nights in the country were no more opaque; half
a century ago no one bothered to light the streets of my village
other than by the aid of large lanterns suspended from the fist
by a ring, reinforced by bars. The divergent shadow of these
bars still sways in my memory, still progresses at my side,
stripes the walls, the dresses of the peasant women, wavers
over the dog's back.

For the dog – whether its name was Domino, Patasson,
Finaud or Lisette – the dog used to accompany us to Midnight
Mass in memory of a night when the ox and the ass received

the gift of speech. He sat in our pew of notables, between Sido my mother and her daughter, without evincing any surprise, listening to the hymns and the harmonium. In the church of my childhood no one has repaired the steeple that was struck by lightning some two centuries ago. But the village prefers it as it is – and so do I.

Returning from Midnight Mass . . . Here I shall stop short if my lady readers were expecting me to record the annals of a day and a night unparalleled in the year. Sido, my mother, never sufficiently nor sufficiently well loved, already saw with terror the growing emptiness of her maternal hands, her barns. So we took care not to ask for what she would not have been able to give us. It is to our credit as children and adolescents that no progeny less grasping than ourselves could have been found. The two boys were happy enough if they had the wherewithal to buy a butterfly-net, two display cases and some long brass pins, nets to fish for crayfish. I was the youngest, yet Sido put a strange trust in me. Will you laugh at me, reader, if I confess that for my seventh Christmas I asked for the complete plays of Labiche . . . and got them?

The following year I was more difficult. I wanted crystal balls and great scintillating tear-drops like those that hung beneath the chandeliers of a nearby château. I gave those up.

But, recollecting this dry-eyed renunciation, you may well believe that on the day when my daughter, at the age of seven, asked at Christmas for corduroy trousers 'like the men who work on the railway-line', she got not only the corduroy breeches but also the red cummerbund, the woollen belt with fringes at each end which goes thrice round the loins.

Parents cannot be too conscious of the fact that, in children, the avowal of a ritual covetous desire is the flower of a long dream, the single phrase which sums up a novel. When a little boy plied with questions resolves to say: 'For New Year I'd like a ruler, some green oil-cloth, and a wire to cut butter . . .', I could wish, parents, that you did not crush with humiliating raillery a dream with its special privacy and romanticism. Give the oil-cloth, the ruler, and the wire to cut butter – your diary-man hardly uses it now, anyway – and on top of that, try when you give them to adopt a shrewd knowledgeable air. It will do a lot for you.

You may find it strange that my childhood Christmases – down there they say '*Nouël*' – lacked the fresh-cut fir tree, the sugared fruits and little lights. But don't feel too sorry for me, our evening of the twenty-fourth was none the less a night of celebrations in our quiet way. It was very rare for Sido not to have found in the garden – surviving full-blown beneath the snow – the flowers of the hellebore which we call Christmas rose. In a bouquet at the centre of the table, their oval closed buds, assailed by the heat of the splendid fire, opened in mechanical fits and starts which alarmed the cats and for which I was as much on the *qui vive* as they were. We had neither black pudding nor white pudding nor turkey with chestnuts, but only the chestnuts boiled and roasted, and Sido's *chef d'oeuvre*, a blancmange studded with three kinds of raisins – Smyrna, Malaga, Corinth – and stuffed with preserved melon, slivers of citron and small dices of orange.

Then, as we were permitted to stay up, the feast continued

as a calm watch-night to the accompaniment of whispering of rustled newspapers, of turned pages, of the fire on which we'd throw some green prunings and a handful of coarse salt which crackled and flamed green on the embers . . .

What, no more than that? No, nothing. None of us desired anything further, or complained of having too little. The howling winter assailed the shutters. The great copper kettle, seated in the ashes, and the clay hot water bottles it was going to fill, promised warm beds in cold rooms . . .

'Mummy, I don't want to go to bed! I want to watch all night, every night! . . .'

'As you wish, Minet-Chéri . . . There's the dawn. You see, the snow's turning blue between the slats of the shutters. Can't you hear the cocks crowing?'

I imagined I was still watching . . . But in fact, surprised by the late hour, I was already asleep, head on my folded arms, my plaits alongside my cheeks like two guardian snakes . . .

Roisin Tierney
(1963–)

Roisin Tierney was born and educated in Dublin, where she took her degree in psychology and philosophy at University College. Since 1985 she has lived in London and worked in a wide variety of positions, ranging from a theatrical make-up artist to an arts administrator and fundraiser. She is also actively involved in the organic farming movement. Her poetry has been published in *Poetry Street, Moonstone*, and *Redbrick Review*. This Christmas poem, 'Apotheosis', was published in *Moonstone* in 2000.

I remember the donkey
When we were small, at midnight mass.
My sisters liked the baby child
Surrounded by the ox and ass
And would squeal coming back in the car
'Oh did you see the baby, did you see the baby'
While I sat there stunned by the donkey
Whose feathery ears were like those of Midas
The golden king, or like Long-ears
Who was stolen away by the King of the Tinkers.
They almost twitched.

In later years
At the local school, a crush of pre-fabs
Set in fields, we learned our books
And more besides – One sunny day
We saw the head nun through the glass
Walking down the narrow path
From the convent. A herd of horses
illegally grazed the lawn. They had been loosed
To eat the grass and break the rules
By travelling folk. With them an ass,
Who sugared by our lunch-time snacks
Downfaced the nun and slowly edged her back
Along the path to her confines
Followed by our laughs and cries
Of 'Freedom!'

Now when I get Christmas cards,
Of frosted robins and evergreens,
Or Bambi in the snow again,
Sometimes an older theme sneaks in;
A donkey marching towards Bethlehem
His pagan mind intent upon
A donkey's reinvention.

Charlotte Brontë
(1816–55)

Charlotte was the eldest of the three celebrated Brontë sisters, but outlived them and her brother Branwell, who all died of tuberculosis. She was born in Yorkshire and moved to Haworth in 1820 when her father became the rector there. Her mother died when the children were young, and they were cared for by their aunt. The Brontë children enjoyed a reasonably happy childhood, although they had few friends. They read avidly and made up stories to entertain each other. In later years their brother Branwell became increasingly dissolute, and the sisters had to work to pay off the debts he incurred. Charlotte worked as a teacher and formed an unreciprocated attachment to the father of her charges when she worked as a governess in Brussels. All three sisters started to write novels and Charlotte's first success was with *Jane Eyre*, which was published under the pseudonym of Currer Bell in 1847. She was an accomplished poet as well as a novelist. Matthew Arnold described her as one whose mind contained 'hunger, rebellion and rage'. She married her father's curate, Arthur Bell Nicholls, in 1854 and died during pregnancy the following year.

This extract from *Jane Eyre* describes an achingly lonely Christmas. It takes place towards the beginning of the book, when the young protagonist is living in misery and deprivation at Gateshead, the home of her rich, uncaring relatives.

Christmas and New Year had been celebrated at Gateshead with the usual festive cheer; presents had been interchanged, dinners and evening parties given. From every enjoyment I was, of course, excluded: my share of the gaiety consisted in witnessing the daily apparelling of Eliza and Georgiana, and seeing them descend to the drawing-room, dressed out in thin muslin frocks and scarlet sashes, with hair elaborately ringletted; and afterwards, in listening to the sound of the piano or the harp played below, to the passing to and fro of the butler and footman, to the jingling of glass and china as refreshments were handed, to the broken hum of conversation as the drawing-room doors opened and closed. When tired of this occupation, I would retire from the stairhead to the solitary and silent nursery: there, though somewhat sad, I was not miserable. To speak truth, I had not the least wish to go into company, for in company I was very rarely noticed; and if Bessie had but been kind and companionable, I should have deemed it a treat to spend the evenings quietly with her, instead of passing them under the formidable eye of Mrs. Reed, in a room full of ladies and gentlemen. But Bessie, as soon as she had dressed her young ladies, used to take herself off to the lively regions of the kitchen and housekeeper's room, generally bearing the candle along with her. I then sat with my doll on my knee, till the fire got low, glancing round occasionally to make sure that nothing worse than myself haunted the shadowy room; and when the embers sank to a dull red, I undressed hastily, tugging at knots and strings as I best might, and sought shelter from cold and darkness in my crib. To this crib I always took my doll; human beings must love something, and in the dearth of worthier objects of affection, I contrived to find a pleasure in loving and cherishing a faded graven image, shabby as a miniature scarecrow. It puzzles me now to remember with what absurd sincerity I doated on this little toy, half fancying it alive and capable of sensation. I could not sleep unless it was folded in my night-gown: and when it lay there safe and warm, I was comparatively happy, believing it to be happy likewise.

Long did the hours seem while I waited the departure of the company, and listened for the sound of Bessie's step on the stairs: sometimes she would come up in the interval to seek her thimble or her scissors, or perhaps to bring me something by way of supper – a bun or a cheese-cake – then she would sit on the bed while I ate it, and when I had finished, she would tuck the clothes round me and twice she kissed me, and said, 'Good night, Miss Jane.' When thus gentle, Bessie seemed to me the best, prettiest, kindest being in the world.

Sue Townsend
(1946–)

Sue Townsend created a J. K. Rowling-style sensation with her books about Adrian Mole, the hormonal teenager. The first book, *The Secret Diary of Adrian Mole Aged 13¾*, appeared in 1982, and became both a play and a television series. Townsend has followed Mole out of agonised adolescence and into an incompetent maturity in a number of sequels. She has published several adult novels, including *Rebuilding Coventry* (1988) and *The Queen and I* (1992), which was adapted for the stage.

This extract comes from *The Secret Diary of Adrian Mole Aged 13¾*. Characters include the love of his life, Pandora, his teacher, Miss Elf, and Bert and Queenie, a pair of pensioners whom Mole has befriended.

Saturday December 19th

I've got no money for Christmas presents. But I have made my Christmas list in case I find ten pounds in the street.

Pandora – Big bottle of Chanel No. 5 (£1.50)
Mother – Egg-timer (75p)
Father – Bookmarker (38p)
Grandma – Packet of J cloths (45p)
Dog – Dog chocolates (45p)
Bert – 20 Woodbines (95p)
Auntie Susan – Tin of Nivea (60p)
Sabre – Box of Bob Martins, small (39p)
Nigel – Family box of Maltesers (34p)
Miss Elf – Oven-glove (home-made)

Wednesday December 23rd

9 a.m. Only two shopping days left for Christmas and I am still penniless. I have made a Blue Peter oven-glove for Miss Elf, but in order to give it to her in time for Christmas I will have to go into the ghetto and risk getting mugged.

I will have to go out carol singing, there is nothing else I can do to raise finance.

10 p.m. Just got back from carol singing. The suburban houses were a dead loss. People shouted, 'Come back at Christmas', without even opening the door. My most appreciative audience were the drunks staggering in and out of the Black Bull. Some of them wept openly at the beauty of my solo rendition of 'Silent Night'. I must say that I presented a touching picture as I stood in the snow with my young face lifted to the heavens ignoring the scenes of drunken revelry around me.

I made £3.13½ plus an Irish tenpence and a Guinness bottletop. I'm going out again tomorrow. I will wear my school uniform, it should be worth a few extra quid.

Thursday December 24th
Took Bert's Woodbines round to the home. Bert is hurt because I haven't been to see him. He said he didn't want to spend Christmas with a lot of malicious old women. Him and Queenie are causing a scandal. They are unofficially engaged. They have got their names on the same ashtray. I have invited Bert and Queenie for Christmas Day. My mother doesn't know yet but I'm sure she won't mind, we have got a big turkey. I sang a few carols for the old ladies. I made two pounds eleven pence out of them so I went to Woolworth's to buy Pandora's Chanel No. 5. They hadn't got any so I bought her an underarm deodorant instead.

The house looks dead clean and sparkling, there is a magic smell of cooking and satsumas in the air. I have searched around for my presents but they are not in the usual places. I want a racing bike, nothing else will please me. It's time I was independently mobile.

11 p.m. Just got back from the Black Bull. Pandora came with me, we wore our school uniforms and reminded all the drunks of their own children. They coughed up conscience money to the tune of twelve pounds fifty-seven! So we are going to see a pantomime on Boxing Day, and we will have a family bar of Cadbury's Diary Milk each!

Friday December 25th
Christmas Day
Got up at 5 a.m. to have a ride on my racing bike. My father
paid for it with American Express. I couldn't ride it far because
of the snow, but it didn't matter. I just like looking at it. My
father had written on the gift tag attached to the handlebars,
'Don't leave it out in the rain this time' – as if I would!

My parents had severe hangovers, so I took them breakfast
in bed and gave them my presents at the same time. My mother
was overjoyed with her egg-timer and my father was equally
delighted with his bookmark, in fact everything was going OK
until I casually mentioned that Bert and Queenie were my
guests for the day, and would my father mind getting out of bed
and picking them up in his car.

The row went on until the lousy Sugdens arrived. My
Grandma and Grandad Sugden and Uncle Dennis and his wife
Marcia and their son Maurice all look the same, as if they went
to funerals every day of their lives. I can hardly believe that my
mother is related to them. The Sugdens refused a drink and had
a cup of tea whilst my mother defrosted the turkey in the bath.
I helped my father carry Queenie (fifteen stone) and Bert (fourteen stone) out of our car. Queenie is one of those loud types of
old ladies who dye their hair and try to look young. Bert is in
love with her. He told me when I was helping him into the
toilet.

Grandma Mole and Auntie Susan came at twelve-thirty and
pretended to like the Sugdens. Auntie Susan told some amusing stories about life in prison but nobody but me and my
father and Bert and Queenie laughed.

I went up to the bathroom and found my mother crying and running the turkey under the hot tap. She said, 'The bloody thing won't thaw out, Adrian. What am I going to do?, I said, 'Just bung it in the oven.' So she did.

We sat down to eat Christmas dinner four hours late. By then my father was too drunk to eat anything. The Sugdens enjoyed the Queen's Speech but nothing else seemed to please them. Grandma Sugden gave me a book called *Bible Stories for Boys*. I could hardly tell her that I had lost my faith, so I said thank-you and wore a false smile for so long that it hurt.

The Sugdens went to their camp beds at ten o'clock. Bert, Queenie and my mother and father played cards while I polished my bike. We all had a good time making jokes about the Sugdens. Then my father drove Bert and Queenie back to the home and I phoned Pandora up and told her that I loved her more than life itself.

I am going round to her house tomorrow to give her the deodorant and escort her to the pantomime.

Saturday December 26th
Bank Holiday in UK and Rep. of Ireland (a day may be given in lieu). **New Moon**
The Sugdens got up at 7 a.m. and sat around in their best clothes looking respectable. I went out on my bike. When I got back my mother was still in bed, and my father was arguing with Grandad Sugden about our dog's behaviour, so I went for another ride.

I called in on Grandma Mole, ate four mince pies, then rode back home. I put my new suede jacket and corduroy trousers on (courtesy of my father's Barclaycard) and called for Pandora; she gave me a bottle of after-shave for my Christmas present. It was a proud moment, it signified the *End of Childhood*.

We quite enjoyed the pantomime but it was rather childish for our taste. Bill Ash and Carole Hayman were good as Aladdin and the Princess, but the robbers played by Jeff Teare and Ian Giles were best. Sue Pomeroy gave a hilarious performance as Widow Twankey. In this she was greatly helped by her cow, played by Chris Martin and Lou Wakefield.

Ntozake Shange
(1948–)

Ntozake Shange is an African-American poet, playwright, dancer, actress, novelist, feminist and educator. She was born Paulette Williams, the daughter of a surgeon and a psychiatric social worker, but she changed what she described as her 'slave name' to Ntozake Shange, which means 'she who comes with her own things' and 'she who walks like a lion' in Xhosa. Her work, which has been both praised and criticised for its unconventional language and structure, explores the difficulties which African-American women confront in their everyday and creative lives. Her books include poetry: *Nappy Edges* (1978) and *A Daughter's Geography* (1983), the novels *Sassafrass, Cypress and Indigo* (1982) and *Betsey Brown* (1985), and her celebrated 'choreopoem' *for colored girls who have considered suicide/when the rainbow is enuf* (1977), a combination of poetry, music, dance and mime which she performed across the United States in schools, workshops, and eventually on Broadway.

This extract from *Sassafrass, Cypress and Indigo* describes an exuberant Christmas in an extraordinary household.

The tree glistened by the front window of the parlor. Hilda Effania had covered it, of course, with cloth & straw. Satin ribbons of scarlet, lime, fuchsia, bright yellow, danced on the far limbs of the pine. Tiny straw angels of dried palm swung from the upper branches. Apples shining, next to candy canes & gingerbread men, brought shouts of joy & memory from the girls, who recognized their own handiwork. The black satin stars with appliqués of the Christ Child Cypress had made when she was ten. Sassafrass fingered the lyres she fashioned for the children singing praises of the little Jesus: little burlap children with lyres she'd been making since she could thread a needle, among the miniatures of Indigo's dolls. Hilda Effania had done something else special for this Christmas, though. In silk frames of varied pastels were the baby pictures of her girls, & one of her wedding day: Hilda Effania & Alfred, November 30, 1946.

Commotion. Rustling papers. Glee & Surprise. Indigo got a very tiny laced brassiere from Cypress. Sassafrass had given her a tiny pair of earrings, dangling golden violins. Indigo had made for both her sisters dolls in their very own likenesses. Both five feet tall, with hips, & bras. Indigo had dressed the dolls in the old clothes Cypress & Sassafrass had left at home.

'Look in their panties,' Indigo blurted. Cypress felt down in her doll's panties. Sassafrass pulled her doll's drawers. They both found velvet sanitary napkins with their names embroidered cross the heart of silk.

'Oh, Indigo. You're kidding. You're not menstruating, are you?'

'Indigo, you got your period?'

'Yes, she did.' Hilda Effania joined, trying to change the subject. She'd known Indigo was making dolls, but not that the dolls had their period.

'Well, what else did you all get?' Hilda asked provocatively.

Cypress pulled out an oddly shaped package wrapped entirely in gold sequins. 'Mama, this is for you.' The next box was embroidered continuously with Sassafrass' name. 'Here, guess whose?' Cypress held Indigo's shoulders. Indigo had on her new bra over her nightgown. Waiting for her mother & sister to open their gifts, Cypress did *tendues*. 'Hold still, Indigo. If you move, my alignment goes off.'

'Oh, Cypress, this is just lovely.' Hilda Effania didn't know what else to say. Cypress had given her a black silk negligée with a very revealing bed jacket. 'I certainly have to think when I could wear this. & you all won't be home to see it.'

'Aw, Mama. Try it on,' Cypress pleaded.

'Yeah, Mama. Put that on. It looks so nasty.' Indigo squinched up her face, giggled.

'Oh, Cypress, these are so beautiful. I can hardly believe it.' Sassafrass held the embroidered box open. In the box lined with beige raw silk were 7 cherrywood hand-carved crochet needles of different gauges.

'Bet not one white girl up to the Callahan School has ever in her white life laid eyes on needles like that!' Cypress hugged her sister, flexed her foot. 'Indigo you got to put that bra on under your clothes, not on top of 'em! Mama, would you look at this little girl?'

Hilda Effania had disappeared. 'I'm trying on this scandalous thing, Cypress. You all look for your notes at the foot of the tree.' She shouted from her bedroom, thinking she looked pretty good for a widow with three most grown girls.

Hilda Effania always left notes for the girls, explaining where their Christmas from Santa was. This practice began the first year Sassafrass had doubted that a fat white man came down her chimney to bring her anything. Hilda solved that problem by leaving notes from Santa Claus for all the children. That way they had to go search the house, high & low, for their gifts. Santa surely had to have been there. Once school chums & reality interfered with this myth, Hilda continued the practice of leaving her presents hidden away. She liked the idea that each child experienced her gift in privacy. The special relationship she nurtured with each was protected from rivalries, jokes & Christmas confusions. Hilda Effania loved thinking that she'd managed to give her daughters a moment of their own.

My Oldest Darling, Sassafrass,
    In the back of the pantry is something from Santa. In a red box by the attic window is something your father would want you to have. Out by the shed in a bucket covered with straw is a gift from your Mama.
        Love to you,
        Mama

Darling Cypress,
    Underneath my hat boxes in the 2nd floor closet is your present from Santa. Look behind the tomatoes I canned last

year for what I got you in your Papa's name. My own choice
for you is under your bed.
XOXOX,
Mama

Sweet Little Indigo,
This is going to be very simple. Santa left you something
outside your violin. I left you a gift by the outdoor stove on
the right hand side. Put your coat on before you go out there.
And the special something I got you from your Daddy is way
up in the china cabinet. Please, be careful.
I love you so much,
Mama

In the back of the pantry between the flour & rice, Sassafrass
found a necklace of porcelain roses. Up in the attic across from
Indigo's mound of resting dolls, there was a red box all right,
with a woven blanket of mohair, turquoise & silver. Yes, her
father would have wanted her to have a warm place to sleep.
Running out to the shed, Sassafrass knocked over the bucket
filled with straw. There on the ground lay eight skeins of her
mother's finest spun cotton, dyed so many colors. Sassafrass sat
out in the air feeling her yarns.

Cypress wanted her mother's present first. Underneath her
bed, she felt tarlatan. A tutu. Leave it to Mama. Once she gathered the whole thing out where she could see it, Cypress started
to cry. A tutu *juponnage*, reaching to her ankles, rose & laven-
der. The waist was a wide sash with the most delicate
needlework she'd ever seen. Tiny toe shoes in white & pink

graced brown ankles tied with ribbons. Unbelievable. Cypress stayed in her room dancing in her tutu till lunchtime. Then she found *The Souls of Black Folks* by DuBois near the tomatoes from her Papa's spirit. She was the only one who'd insisted on calling him Papa, instead of Daddy or Father. He didn't mind. So she guessed he wouldn't mind now. 'Thank you so much, Mama & Papa.' Cypress slowly went to the 2nd floor closet where she found Santa'd left her a pair of opal earrings. To thank her mother Cypress did a complete *port de bras*, in the Cecchetti manner, by her mother's vanity. The mirrors inspired her.

Indigo had been very concerned that anything was near her fiddle that she hadn't put there. Looking at her violin, she knew immediately what her gift from Santa was. A brand-new case. No second-hand battered thing from Uncle John. Indigo approached her instrument slowly. The case was of crocodile skin, lined with white velvet. Plus, Hilda Effania had bought new rosin, new strings. Even cushioned the fiddle with cleaned raw wool. Indigo carried her new case with her fiddle outside to the stove where she found a music stand holding *A Practical Method for Violin* by Nicolas Laoureux. 'Oh, my. She's right about that. Mama would be real mad if I never learned to read music.' Indigo looked thru the pages, understanding nothing. Whenever she was dealing with something she didn't under-stand, she made it her business to learn. With great difficulty, she carried her fiddle, music stand, & music book into the house. Up behind the wine glasses that Hilda Effania rarely used, but dusted regularly, was a garnet bracelet from the memory of her father. Indigo figures the bracelet weighed so little, she would definitely be able to wear it every time she played her fiddle. Actually, she could wear it while conversing with the Moon.

Hilda Effania decided to chance fate & spend the rest of the morning in her fancy garb from Cypress. The girls were silent when she entered the parlor in the black lace. She looked like she did in those hazy photos from before they were born. Indigo rushed over to the easy chair & straightened the pillows.

'Mama, I have my present for you.' Hilda Effania swallowed hard. There was no telling what Indigo might bring her.

'Well, Sweetheart. I'm eager for it. I'm excited, too.'

Indigo opened her new violin case, took out her violin, made motions of tuning it (which she'd already done). In a terribly still moment, she began 'My Buddy,' Hilda Effania's mother's favorite song. At the end, she bowed to her mother. Her sisters applauded.

Sassafrass gave her mother two things: a woven hanging of twined ikat using jute and raffia, called 'You Know Where We Came From, Mama'; & six amethysts with holes drilled thru, for her mother's creative weaving.

'Mama, you've gotta promise me you won't have a bracelet, or a ring or something made from them. Those are for your very own pieces.' Sassafrass wanted her mother to experience weaving as an expression of herself, not as something the family did for Miz Fitzhugh. Hilda Effania was still trying to figure out where in the devil she could put this 'hanging,' as Sassafrass called it.

'Oh, no dear. I wouldn't dream of doing anything with these stones but what you intended.'

When the doorbell rang, Hilda Effania didn't know what to do with herself. Should she run upstairs? Sit calmly? Run get her house robe? She had no time to do any of that. Indigo opened the door.

'Merry Christmas, Miz Fitzhugh. Won't you come in?' Hilda sank back in the easy chair. Cypress casually threw her mother an afghan to cover herself. Miz Fitzhugh in red wool suit, tailored green satin shirt, red tam, all Hilda's design, and those plain brown pumps white women like, wished everyone a 'Merry Christmas.' She said Mathew, her butler, would bring some sweetbreads & venison over later, more toward the dinner hour. Miz Fitzhugh liked Sassafrass the best of the girls. That's why she'd sponsored her at the Callahan School. The other two, the one with the gall to want to be a ballerina & the headstrong one with the fiddle, were much too much for Miz Fitzhugh. They didn't even wanta be weavers. What was becoming of the Negro, refusing to ply an honorable trade.

Nevertheless, Miz Fitzhugh hugged each one with her frail blue-veined arms, gave them their yearly checks for their savings accounts she'd established when each was born. There be no talk that her Negroes were destitute. What she didn't know was that Hilda Effania let the girls use that money as they pleased. Hilda believed every family needed only one mother. She was the mother to her girls. That white lady was mighty generous, but she wasn't her daughters' mama or manna from Heaven. If somebody needed taking care of, Hilda Effania determined that was her responsibility; knowing in her heart that white folks were just peculiar.

'Why Miz Fitzhugh, that's right kindly of you,' Hilda honeyed.

'Why Hilda, you know I feel like the girls were my very own,' Miz Fitzhugh confided. Cypress began a series of violent *ronds de jambe*. Sassafrass picked up all the wrapping papers as if it were the most important thing in the world. Indigo felt some huge anger coming over her. Next thing she knew, Miz Fitzhugh couldn't keep her hat on. There was a wind justa pushing, blowing Miz Fitzhugh out the door. Because she had blue blood or blue veins, whichever, Indigo knew Miz Fitzhugh would never act like anything strange was going on. She'd let herself be blown right out the door with her white kid gloves, red tailored suit, & all. Waving good-bye, shouting, 'Merry Christmas,' Miz Fitzhugh vanished as demurely as her station demanded. Sucha raucous laughing & carrying on rarely came out of Hilda Effania's house like it did after Miz Fitzhugh'd been blown away. Hilda Effania did an imitation of her, hugging the girls.

'But Miz Fitzhugh, do the other white folks know you touch your Negroes?' Hilda responded, 'Oh, I don't tell anyone!'

christmas at our place

The Starkadders, of Cold Comfort Farm, had never got the hang of Christmas, somehow, and on Boxing Day there was always a run on the Howling Pharmacy for lint, bandages, and boracic powder.

STELLA GIBBONS

George Sand
(Amantine Aurore Dudevant)
(1804–76)

George Sand was born in Paris, the illegitimate daughter of
Marshal de Saxe. She married Casimir, Baron Dudevant at the
age of 18, but left him after nine years, taking her two children
with her. Sand scandalised French society with her unconventional ways and love affairs, with the composer Chopin and the
writer de Musset, amongst others. After her separation from
her husband she permanently adopted the name George Sand
under which all her numerous works – novels, plays and letters – were published. The novelist Gustave Flaubert was one
of the many famous men with whom she enjoyed a lifelong
friendship. Although Flaubert was 17 years her junior, it was
Sand who helped him cope with the suffering and depression
his ageing caused him.

In this letter, written in 1869, she urges him to join the
Christmas festivities at her home, Nohant. It is typical of the
tone of all her correspondence – imperious, detailed and
humorous.

Nohant, December 18th, 1869.

. . . Women are joining with men in denouncing your work! Come then and forget that persecution in our midst, far away from the turmoil of literary and Parisian life; or, rather, come and rejoice over it; for such unkindly treatment is the unavoidable lot of all those who possess worth and talent. You must bear in mind that all those who are speared are only fit to be Academicians.

Our letters crossed each other. In mine, I requested you, I now still request you, to come, not on Christmas Eve, but on the day before in order to keep up the réveillon* with us on the night of the 24th. This is the intended programme: We dine at six precisely, we shall then make up the Christmas tree and play the marionettes for the children, in order that they may go to bed at nine. After that, we chat and sup at twelve pm. The coach does not reach here before half past six at the earliest; therefore that would deprive the little ones of their pleasure, as you could not reach here before late. You must therefore, start on Tuesday, the 23rd, at nine in the morning, so that we may see and kiss one another to our hearts' content, and not see the joy of your arrival disturbed by the requests of imperious and excited children.

You must stay with us very long, very long; on New Year's Day and On Twelfth Day we will again indulge in follies. Ours is a stupid but happy roof, and now is the time of our

---

* The festivity kept up by French people on returning home from midnight mass with which Christmas day is ushered in.

recreation after work. I will to-night finish my task for this year. It would indeed be my reward to see you, beloved, dear, old friend: do not refuse it to me.

G. Sand.

Edith Sitwell
(1887–1964)

Edith Sitwell was born in Scarborough, Yorkshire. When she became financially independent at the age of 27, she moved to London, but she was plagued by ill health and money problems and spent periods in Paris, where the cost of living was lower. She was a flamboyant and eccentric character, adopting on occasion Elizabethan dress and given to extreme opinions, which she was not afraid to express. In addition to poetry, Sitwell wrote several volumes of critical essays, biography, autobiography, social history and fiction. Her best-known work is her experimental book of poetry, *Façade*, which was published in 1922 and set to music by Sir William Walton. In 1954 she was made a Dame Grand Cross of the British Empire; the same year she became a Roman Catholic.

Her correspondence with many of the literary and bohemian figures of the day shows a woman with a delightful sense of the ridiculous. This letter, written in 1933, is to Rée Gorer, mother of Geoffrey and Peter Gorer. Geoffrey was an anthropologist; all three were part of Sitwell's circle. The 'Pavlik' of the letter is the homosexual Russian painter Pavel Tchelitchew, with whom Sitwell fell in love. Allen Tanner, a pianist, was one of Pavlik's lovers. Edith herself was forced to assume the role of platonic muse and patron. Osbert is her brother, Osbert Sitwell, also a writer. 'Sachie' is their brother Sacheverell, art critic and poet.

During this time Edith was working on her books *The English Eccentrics* (1933) and *Victoria of England* (1936). In a later letter to a friend, she described herself as 'a bad Christmasser', claiming that she was always condemned to look after deaf old ladies and then left by her father in complete solitude, forgotten and uncared for.

129 Rue Saint-Dominique
Paris VIIe
[December 1933]

My dear Rée,

. . . I've just had, between ourselves (and, naturally Geoffrey and Peter) the most perfect experience with Allen. I've only been to their flat twice or three times since my return, because Pavlik is much occupied, and I think Russians only *really* like idiots, prostitutes and dressmakers – preferably people who are all three in one. However, he is now relenting a little towards me, because it is obvious that if my life goes on in this way much longer, I *shall* be an idiot (or at least mad), even if I can't attain to the other ideals. So I asked the whole family to dine with me on Christmas night. They accepted. But ten days after, I got a letter from Allen saying could I have them to lunch instead, or, alternatively, he would arrange to take me to the house of a dear American friend of his for dinner, as this gentleman had now invited them to dine on Christmas night, and he thought they would go there!! He did this, I may say, without Pavlik's knowledge. I have been extremely firm, not to say cross, and have said that I am not in the habit of going to strangers' houses for my dinner at Christmas.

I saw Osbert on his way to Pekin. His dear old father has now cut him and Sachie out of his will, and has left a codicil saying how badly and vilely we have all behaved. We shan't know *what* we've done until the old gentleman dies and the will is read. But may that day be soon, for I confess to curiosity on the point . . .

Stella Gibbons
(1902–89)

Stella Gibbons was born in London. As a child she used to entertain her brothers by making up stories. She trained as a journalist and worked in Fleet Street for ten years before turning her attention to fiction. She wrote several witty novels, the most famous of which is *Cold Comfort Farm* (1932), a parody of melodramatic novels on rural life, such as those written by Mary Webb. It won the Femina Vie Heureuse Prize. Gibbons also wrote poetry and short stories, including the following, 'Christmas at Cold Comfort Farm'. Published in 1940, the story is a kind of prequel to *Cold Comfort Farm*. All the familiar characters from the novel are seen here, in the days before they were civilised by their cousin, Flora Poste.

It was Christmas Eve. Dusk, a filthy mantle, lay over Sussex when the Reverend Silas Hearsay, Vicar of Howling, set out to pay his yearly visit to Cold Comfort Farm. Earlier in the afternoon he had feared he would not be Guided to go there, but then he had seen a crate of British Port-type wine go past the Vicarage on the grocer's boy's bicycle, and it could only be going, by that road, to the farmhouse. Shortly afterwards he was Guided to go, and set out upon his bicycle.

The Starkadders, of Cold Comfort Farm, had never got the hang of Christmas, somehow, and on Boxing Day there was always a run on the Howling Pharmacy for lint, bandages, and boracic powder. So the Vicar was going up there, as he did every year, to show them the ropes a bit. (It must be explained that these events took place some years before the civilizing hand of Flora Poste had softened and reformed the Farm and its rude inhabitants.)

After removing two large heaps of tussocks which blocked the lane leading to the Farm and thereby releasing a flood of muddy, icy water over his ankles, the Vicar wheeled his machine on towards the farmhouse, reflecting that those tussocks had never fallen there from the dung-cart of Nature. It was clear that someone did not want him to come to the place. He pushed his bicycle savagely up the hill, muttering.

The farmhouse was in silence and darkness. He pulled the ancient hell-bell (once used to warn excommunicated persons to stay away from Divine Service) hanging outside the front door, and waited.

For a goodish bit nothing happened. Suddenly a window far above his head was flung open and a voice wailed into the twilight –

'No! No! No!'

And the window slammed shut again.

'You're making a mistake, I'm sure,' shouted the Vicar, peering up into the webby thongs of the darkness. 'It's me. The Rev Silas Hearsay.'

There was a pause. Then –

'Beant you postman?' asked the voice, rather embarrassed.

'No, no, of course not; come, come!' laughed the Vicar, grinding his teeth.

'I be comin',' retorted the voice. 'Thought it were postman after his Christmas Box.' The window slammed again. After a very long time indeed the door suddenly opened and there stood Adam Lambsbreath, oldest of the farm servants, peering up at the Reverend Hearsay by the light of a lonely rushdip (so called because you dipped it in grease and rushed to wherever you were going before it went out).

'Is anyone at home? May I enter?' enquired the Vicar, entering, and staring scornfully round the desolate kitchen, at the dead blue ashes in the grate, the thick dust on hanch and beam, the feathers blowing about like fun everywhere. Yet even here there were signs of Christmas, for a withered branch of holly stood in a shapeless vessel on the table. And Adam himself . . . there was something even more peculiar than usual about him.

'Are you ailing, man?' asked the Vicar irritably, kicking a chair out of the way and perching himself on the edge of the table.

'Nay, Rev, I be niver better,' piped the old man. '*The older the berry, The more it makes merry*.'

'Then why,' thundered the Vicar, sliding off the table and walking on tiptoe towards Adam with his arms held at full length above his head, 'are you wearing three of Mrs Starkadder's red shawls?'

Adam stood his ground.

'I mun have a red courtepy, master. Can't be Santa Claus wi'out a red courtepy,' he said. 'Iverybody knows that. Ay, the hand o' Fate lies heavy on us all, Christmas and all the year round alike, but I thought I'd bedight meself as Santa Claus, so I did, just to please me little Elfine. And this night at midnight I be goin' around fillin' the stockin's, if I'm spared.'

The Vicar laughed contemptuously.

'So that were why I took three o' Mrs Starkadder's red shawls,' concluded Adam.

'I suppose you have never thought of God in terms of Energy? No, it is too much to expect.' The Reverend Hearsay re-seated himself on the table and glanced at his watch. 'Where in Energy's name is everybody? I have to be at the Assembly Rooms to read a paper on *The Future of The Father Fixation* at eight, and I've got to feed first. If nobody's coming, I'd rather go.'

'Won't ee have a dram o' swede wine first?' a deep voice asked, and a tall woman stepped over the threshold, followed by a little girl of twelve or so with yellow hair and clear, beautiful features. Judith Starkadder dropped her hat on the floor and leant against the table staring listlessly at the Vicar.

'No swede wine, I thank you,' snapped the Reverend Hearsay. He glanced keenly round the kitchen in search of the British Port-type, but there was no sign of it. 'I came up to discuss an article with you and yours. An article in *Home Anthropology*.'

"Twere good of ee, Reverend,' she said tiredly.

'It is called *Christmas: From Religious Festival to Shopping Orgy*. Puts the case for Peace and Good Will very sensibly. Both good for trade. What more can you want?'

'Nothing,' she said, leaning her head on her hand.

'But I see,' the Vicar went on furiously, in a low tone and glaring at Adam, 'that here, as everywhere else, the usual childish wish-fantasies are in possession. Stars, shepherds, mangers, stockings, fir-trees, puddings. Energy help you all! I wish you good night, and a prosperous Christmas.'

He stamped out of the kitchen, and slammed the door after him with such violence that he brought a slate down on his back tyre and cut it open, and he had to walk home, arriving there too late for supper before setting out for Godmere.

After he had gone, Judith stared into the fire without speaking, and Adam busied himself with scraping the mould from a jar of mincemeat and picking some things which had fallen into it out of a large crock of pudding which he had made yesterday.

Elfine, meanwhile, was slowly opening a small brown paper parcel which she had been nursing, and at last revealed a small and mean-looking doll dressed in a sleazy silk dress and one under-garment that did not take off. This she gently nursed, talking to it in a low, sweet voice.

'Who gave you that, child?' asked her mother idly.

'I told you, mother. Uncle Micah and Aunt Rennett and Aunt Prue and Uncle Harkaway and Uncle Ezra.'

'Treasure it. You will not get many such.'

'I know, mother; I do. I love her very much, dear, dear Caroline,' and Elfine gently put a kiss on the doll's face.

'Now, missus, have ee got the Year's Luck? Can't make puddens wi'out the Year's Luck,' said Adam, shuffling forward.

'It's somewhere here. I forget –'

She turned her shabby handbag upside down, and there fell out on the table the following objects:

A small coffin-nail.

A menthol cone.

Three bad sixpences.

A doll's cracked looking-glass.

A small roll of sticking-plaster.

Adam collected these objects and ranged them by the pudding basin.

'Ay, them's all there,' he muttered. 'Him as gets the sticking-plaster'll break a limb; the menthol cone means as you'll be blind wi' headache, the bad coins means as you'll lose all yer money, and him as gets the coffin-nail will die before the New Year. The mirror's seven years' bad luck for someone. Aie! In ye go, curse ye!' and he tossed the objects into the pudding, where they were not easily nor long distinguishable from the main mass.

'Want a stir, missus? Come, Elfine, my popelot, stir long, stir firm, your meat to earn,' and he handed her the butt of an old rifle, once used by Fig Starkadder in the Gordon Riots.

Judith turned from the pudding with what is commonly described as a gesture of loathing, but Elfine took the rifle butt and stirred the mixture once or twice.

'Ay, now tes all mixed,' said the old man, nodding with sat-isfaction. 'To-morrer we'll boil un fer a good hour, and un'll be done.'

'Will an hour be enough?' said Elfine. 'Mrs Hawk-Monitor up at Hautcouture Hall boils hers for eight hours, and another four on Christmas Day.'

'How do ee know?' demanded Adam. 'Have ee been runnin' wi' that young goosepick Mus' Richard again?'

'You shut up. He's awfully decent.'

'Tisn't decent to run wi' a young popelot all over the Downs in all weathers.' ———

'Well, it isn't any of your business, so shut up.'

After an offended pause, Adam said:

'Well, niver fret about puddens. None of 'em here has iver tasted any puddens but mine, and they won't know no differ-ent.'

At midnight, when the farmhouse was in darkness save for the faint flame of a nightlight burning steadily beside the bed of Harkaway, who was afraid of bears, a dim shape might have been seen moving stealthily along the corridor from bedroom to bedroom. It wore three red shawls pinned over its torn nightshirt and carried over its shoulder a nose-bag, (the prop-erty of Viper the gelding), distended with parcels. It was Adam, bent on putting into the stockings of the Starkadders the pres-ents which he had made or bought with his savings. The presents were chiefly swedes, beetroots, mangel-wurzels and turnips, decorated with coloured ribbons and strips of silver paper from tea packets.

'Ay,' muttered the old man, as he opened the door of the room where Meriam, the hired girl, was sleeping over the Christmas week. 'An apple for each will make 'em retch, a couple o' nuts will warm their wits.'

The next instant he stepped back in astonishment. There was a light in the room and there, sitting bolt upright in bed beside her slumbering daughter, was Mrs Beetle.

Mrs Beetle looked steadily at Adam, for a minute or two. Then she observed:

'Some 'opes.'

'Nay, niver say that, soul,' protested Adam, moving to the bedrail where hung a very fully-fashioned salmon-pink silk stocking with ladders all down it. "Tisn't so. E do know well that I looks on the maidy as me own child.'

Mrs Beetle gave a short laugh and adjusted a curler. 'You better not let Agony 'ear you, 'intin' I dunno wot,' said Mrs Beetle. "Urry up and put yer rubbish in there, I want me sleep out; I got to be up at cock-wake ter-morrer.'

Adam put a swede, an apple and a small pot in the stocking and was tip-toeing away when Mrs Beetle, raising her head from the pillow, inquired:

'Wot's that you've give 'er?'

'Eye-shadow,' whispered Adam hoarsely, turning at the door.

'Wot?' hissed Mrs Beetle, inclining her head in an effort to hear. "Ave you gorn crackers?'

'Eye-shadow. To put on the maidy's eyes. 'Twill give that touch o'glamour as be irresistible; it do say so on pot.'

'Get out of 'ere, you old trouble-maker! Don't she 'ave enough bother resistin' as it is, and then you go and give 'er . . .

'ere, wait till I –' and Mrs Beetle was looking around for something to throw as Adam hastily retreated.

'And I'll lay you ain't got no present fer me, ter make matters worse,' she called after him.

Silently he placed a bright new tin of beetle-killer on the washstand and shuffled away.

His experiences in the apartments of the other Starkadders were no more fortunate, for Seth was busy with a friend and was so furious at being interrupted that he threw his riding-boots at the old man, Luke and Mark had locked their door and could be heard inside roaring with laughter at Adam's discomfiture, and Amos was praying, and did not even get up off his knees or open his eyes as he discharged at Adam the goat-pistol which he kept ever by his bed. And everybody else had such enormous holes in their stockings that the small presents Adam put in them fell through on to the floor along with the big ones, and when the Starkadders got up in the morning and rushed round to the foot of the bed to see what Santa had brought, they stubbed their toes on the turnips and swedes and walked on the smaller presents and smashed them to smithereens.

So what with one thing and another everybody was in an even worse temper than usual when the family assembled round the long table in the kitchen for the Christmas dinner about half-past two the next afternoon. They would all have sooner been in some place else, but Mrs Ada Doom (Grandmother Doom, known as Grummer) insisted on them all being there, and as they did not want her to go mad and bring disgrace on the House of Starkadder, there they had to be.

One by one they came in, the men from the fields with soil on their boots, the women fresh from hennery and duck filch with eggs in their bosoms that they gave to Mrs Beetle who was just making the custard. Everybody had to work as usual on Christmas Day, and no one had troubled to put on anything handsomer than their usual workaday clouts stained with mud and plough-oil. Only Elfine wore a cherry-red jersey over her dark shirt and had pinned a spray of holly on herself. An aunt, a distant aunt named Mrs Poste, who lived in London, had unexpectedly sent her the pretty jersey. Prue and Letty had stuck sixpenny artificial posies in their hair, but they only looked wild and queer.

At last all were seated and waiting for Ada Doom.

'Come, come, mun we stick here like jennets i' the trave?' demanded Micah at last. 'Amos, Reuben, do ee carve the turkey. If so be as we wait much longer, 'twill be shent, and the sausages, too.'

Even as he spoke, heavy footsteps were heard approaching the head of the stairs, and everybody at once rose to their feet and looked towards the door.

The low-ceilinged room was already half in dusk, for it was a cold, still Christmas Day, without much light in the grey sky, and the only other illumination came from the dull fire, half-buried under a tass of damp kindling.

Adam gave a last touch to the pile of presents, wrapped in hay and tied with bast, which he had put round the foot of the withered thorn-branch that was the traditional Starkadder Christmas-tree, hastily rearranged one of the tufts of sheep's-wool that decorated its branches, straightened the raven's skeleton that adorned its highest branch in place of a fairy-doll or star, and shuffled into his place just as Mrs Doom reached the foot of the stairs, leaning on her daughter Judith's arm. Mrs Doom struck at him with her stick in passing as she went slowly to the head of the table.

'Well, well. What are we waiting for? Are you all mis-hooden?' she demanded impatiently as she seated herself. 'Are you all here? All? Answer me!' banging her stick.

'Ay, Grummer,' rose the low, dreary drone from all sides of the table. 'We be all here.'

'Where's Seth?' demanded the old woman, peering sharply on either side of the long row.

'Gone out,' said Harkaway briefly, shifting a straw in his mouth.

'What for?' demanded Mrs Doom.

There was an ominous silence.

'He said he was going to fetch something, Grandmother,' at last said Elfine.

'Ay. Well, well, no matter, so long as he comes soon. Amos, carve the bird. Ay, would it were a vulture, 'twere more fitting! Reuben, fling these dogs the fare my bounty provides. Sausages . . . pah! Mince-pies . . . what a black-bitter mockery it all is! Every almond, every raisin, is wrung from the dry, dying soil and paid for with sparse greasy notes grudged alike by bank and buyer. Come, Ezra, pass the ginger wine! Be gay, spawn! Laugh, stuff yourselves, gorge and forget, you rat-heaps! Rot you all!' and she fell back in her chair, gasping and keeping one eye on the British Port-type that was now coming up the table.

'Tes one of her bad days,' said Judith tonelessly. 'Amos, will you pull a cracker wi' me? We were lovers . . . once.'

'Hush, woman.' He shrank back from the proffered treat. 'Tempt me not wi' motters and paper caps. Hell is paved wi' such.' Judith smiled bitterly and fell silent.

Reuben, meanwhile, had seen to it that Elfine got the best bit off the turkey (which is not saying much) and had filled her glass with Port-type wine and well-water.

The turkey gave out before it got to Letty, Prue, Susan, Phœbe, Jane and Rennett, who were huddled together at the foot of the table, and they were making do with brussels-sprouts as hard as bullets drenched with weak gravy, and home-brewed braket. There was silence in the kitchen except for the sough of swallowing, the sudden suck of drinking.

'WHERE IS SETH?' suddenly screamed Mrs Doom, flinging down her turkey-leg and glaring round.

Silence fell; everyone moved uneasily, not daring to speak in case they provoked an outburst. But at that moment the cheerful, if unpleasant, noise of a motor-cycle was heard outside, and in another moment it stopped at the kitchen door. All eyes were turned in that direction, and in another moment in came Seth.

'Well, Grummer! Happen you thought I was lost!' he cried impudently, peeling off his boots and flinging them at Meriam, the hired girl, who cowered by the fire gnawing a sausage skin.

Mrs Doom silently pointed to his empty seat with the turkey-leg, and he sat down.

'She hev had an outhees. Ay, 'twas terrible,' reproved Judith in a low tone as Seth seated himself beside her.

'Niver mind, I ha' something here as will make her chirk like a mellet,' he retorted, and held up a large brown paper parcel. 'I ha' been to the Post Office to get it.'

'Ah, gie it me! Aie, my lost pleasurings! Tes none I get, nowadays; gie it me now!' cried the old woman eagerly.

'Nay, Grummer. Ee must wait till pudden time,' and the young man fell on his turkey ravenously.

When everyone had finished, the women cleared away and poured the pudding into a large dusty dish, which they bore to the table and set before Judith.

'Amos? Pudding?' she asked listlessly. 'In a glass or on a plate?'

'On plate, on plate, woman,' he said feverishly bending forward with a fierce glitter in his eye. 'Tes easier to see the Year's Luck so.'

A stir of excitement now went through the company, for everybody looked forward to seeing everybody else drawing ill-luck from the symbols concealed in the pudding. A fierce, attentive silence fell. It was broken by a wail from Reuben –

'The coin – the coin! Wala wa!' and he broke into deep, heavy sobs. He was saving up to buy a tractor, and the coin meant, of course, that he would lose all his money during the year.

'Never mind, Reuben, dear,' whispered Elfine, slipping an arm round his neck. 'You can have the penny father gave me.'

Shrieks from Letty and Prue now announced that they had received the menthol cone and the sticking-plaster, and a low mutter of approval greeted the discovery by Amos of the broken mirror.

Now there was only the coffin-nail, and a ghoulish silence fell on everybody as they dripped pudding from their spoons in a feverish hunt for it; Ezra was running his through a tea-strainer.

But no one seemed to have got it.

'Who has the coffin-nail? Speak, you draf-saks!' at last demanded Mrs Doom.

'Not I.' 'Nay.' 'Niver sight nor snitch of it,' chorussed everybody.

'Adam!' Mrs Doom turned to the old man. 'Did you put the coffin-nail into the pudding?'

'Ay, mistress, that I did – didn't I, Mis' Judith, didn't I, Elfine, my liddle lovesight?'

'He speaks truth for once, mother.'

'Yes, he did, Grandmother. I saw him.'

'*Then where is it?*' Mrs Doom's voice was low and terrible and her gaze moved slowly down the table, first on one side and then the other, in search of signs of guilt, while everyone cowered over their plates.

Everyone, that is, except Mrs Beetle, who continued to eat a sandwich that she had taken out of a cellophane wrapper, with every appearance of enjoyment.

'Carrie Beetle!' shouted Mrs Doom.

'I'm 'ere,' said Mrs Beetle.

'Did you take the coffin-nail out of the pudding?'

'Yes, I did.' Mrs Beetle leisurely finished the last crumb of sandwich and wiped her mouth with a clean handkerchief. 'And will again, if I'm spared till next year.'

'You . . . you . . . you . . .' choked Mrs Doom, rising in her chair and beating the air with her clenched fists. 'For two hundred years . . . Starkadders . . . coffin-nails in puddings . . . and now . . . you . . . dare . . .'

'Well, I 'ad enough of it las' year,' retorted Mrs Beetle. 'That pore old soul Earnest Dolour got it, as well you may remember –'

. . . After a minute's uneasy silence –

'Grummer.' Seth bent winningly towards the old woman, the large brown paper parcel in his hand. 'Will you see your present now?'

'Aye, boy, aye. Let me see it. You're the only one that has thought of me, the only one.'

Seth was undoing the parcel, and now revealed a large book, handsomely bound in red leather with gilt lettering.

'There, Grummer. 'Tis the year's numbers o' *The Milk Producers' Weekly Bulletin and Cowkeepers' Guide*. I collected un for ee, and had un bound. Art pleased?'

'Ay. 'Tis handsome enough. A graceful thought,' muttered the old lady, turning the pages. Most of them were pretty battered, owing to her habit of rolling up the paper and hitting anyone with it who happened to be within reach. "Tis better so. 'Tis heavier. Now I can *throw* it.'

The Starkadders so seldom saw a clean and handsome object at the farmhouse (for Seth was only handsome) that they now crept round, fascinated, to examine the book with murmurs of awe. Among them came Adam, but no sooner had he bent over the book then he recoiled from it with a piercing scream.

'Aie! . . . aie! aie!'

'What's the matter, dotard?' screamed Mrs Doom, jabbing at him with the volume. 'Speak you kaynard!'

'Tes calf! Tes bound in calf! And tes our Pointless's calf, as she had last Lammastide, as was sold at Godmere to Farmer Lust!' cried Adam, falling to the floor. At the same instant, Luke hit Micah in the stomach, Harkaway pushed Ezra into the fire, Mrs Doom flung the bound volume of *The Milk Producers' Weekly Bulletin and Cowkeepers' Guide* at the struggling mass, and the Christmas dinner collapsed into indescribable confusion.

Jane Welsh Carlyle
(1801–66)

Jane Baillie Welsh was 25 years old when she married the historian Thomas Carlyle in 1926. The couple lived on her family estate in Scotland. She refused to become a writer, in spite of her husband's encouragement, and spent most of her life nursing him through his illnesses and depressions. She is remembered for her vivid and entertaining letters and diaries, which Thomas Carlyle edited and published after her death in 1883. In the following letter, Jane Carlyle describes an extraordinary Christmas party at the home of the great actor Macready, in the hectic company of such luminaries as Charles Dickens and William Makepeace Thackeray. John Welsh, Jane's maternal uncle, had two daughters, Helen and Jeannie. The latter, nicknamed 'Babbie', though 18 years younger than Jane, was a true intimate until her marriage in 1853. It was to Jeannie Welsh that this entertaining letter was sent.

Thursday (23rd Dec., 1843).

A thousand thanks my darling for your long good Christmas letter and also for the *prospective foot-stools*, anything like a *worthy* answer you have small chance of getting from me to-day or any day *this* week. I have just had to swallow a bumper of my uncle's Madeira (which *is* capital drink!) to nerve me for writing at all! A huge boxful of dead animals from the Welshman* arriving late on Saturday night together with the visions of *Scrooge* – had so worked on Carlyle's nervous organisation that he has been seized with a perfect *convulsion* of hospitality, and has actually insisted on *improvising two* dinner parties with only a day between – now the *improvisation* of dinner parties is all very well for the parties who have to *eat* them simply, but for those who have to *organise* them and *help to cook them c'est autre chose ma chère!* I do not remember that I have ever sustained a moment of greater embarrassment in life than yesterday when Helen suggested to me that *I* had better *stuff the turkey* – as she had *forgotten* all about it! *I* had never *known* 'about it'! but as I make it a rule never to exhibit *ignorance* on *any* subject '*devant les domestiques*' for fear of losing their respect – I proceeded to *stuff* the turkey with the same air of calm self dependence with which I told her some time ago, when she applied to me, the whole history of the Scotch freechurch dissensions – which up to this hour I have never been able to *take in!* 'Fortune favours the brave' – the *stuffing* proved pleasanter to the taste than any stuffing I ever remember to

---

* Mr Redwood, a friend of the Carlyles.

have eaten – perhaps it was made with quite new ingredients! –
I do now know! Yesterday I had hare soup – *the* Turkey – stewed
mutton – a bread pudding and mince-pies – with Mrs Allan
Cunningham, Miss Cunningham – and Major Burns (son of
the Poet) to eat thereof. On Monday hare soup – roasted *Welsh*
mutton, stewed beef, ditto pudding, ditto pies – with Robertson,
and John Carlyle, and *the disappointment* of Darwin – and all
that day, to add to my difficulties, I had a headache – so bad that
I should have been in bed if I had not had to stay up to help
Helen – whose faculties get rusted by disuse. On Tuesday
evening I was engaged to assist at Nina Macready's birthday
party – but felt so little up to gaieties on the Monday that I had
resolved to send an apology *as usual* when voilà – on the morning of the appointed day arrives a note from Mrs Macready
imploring me almost with tears in its eyes not to disappoint her
and her 'poor little daughter' by sending an apology – that a well
aired *bed* was prepared for me &c. &c., – this forestalling of my
cruel purpose was successful – I felt that I *must* go *for once* . . .
In fact I was very ill – had been *off* my sleep for a week and felt
as if this night must almost finish me. But little does one know
in this world what will *finish* them or what will *set them up*
again. I question if a long course of mercury would have acted
so beneficially on my liver as this party which I had gone to
with a sacred shudder! But then it was the *very* most agreeable
party that ever I was at in London – everybody there seemed
animated with one purpose to make up to Mrs Macready and
her children for the absence of 'the Tragic Actor' and so amiable
a purpose produced the most joyous results. Dickens and
Forster above all exerted themselves till the perspiration was

pouring down and they seemed *drunk* with their efforts! Only think of that excellent Dickens playing the *conjuror* for one whole hour – the *best* conjuror I ever saw – (and I have paid money to see several) – and Forster acting as his servant. This part of the entertainment concluded with a plum pudding made out of raw flour, raw eggs – all the raw usual ingredients – boiled in a gentleman's hat – and tumbled out reeking – all in one minute before the eyes of the astonished children and astonished grown people! that trick – and his other of changing ladies' pocket handkerchiefs into comfits – and a box full of bran into a box full of – a live guinea-pig! would enable him to make a handsome subsistence let the bookseller trade go as it please – ! Then the dancing – old Major Burns with his one eye – old Jerdan of the Literary Gazette, (escaped out of the Rules of the Queen's Bench for the great occasion!) the gigantic Thackeray &c. &c. all capering like *Maenades!!* Dickens did all but go down on his knees to make *me* – waltz with him! But I thought I did my part well enough in talking the maddest nonsense with *him*, Forster, Thackeray and Maclise – without attempting the Impossible – however *after supper* when we were all madder than ever with the pulling of crackers, the drinking of champagne, and the making of speeches; a universal country dance was proposed – and Forster *seizing me round the waist*, whirled me into the thick of it, and *made* me dance!! like a person in the tread-mill who must move forward or be crushed to death! Once I cried out 'oh for the love of Heaven let me go! you are going to dash my brains out against the folding doors!' to which he answered – (you can fancy his tone) – 'your *brains!!* who cares about their brains *here? let them go!*'

In fact the thing was rising into something not unlike the *rape of the Sabines!* (*Mrs Reid* was happily gone some time) when somebody looked [at] her watch and exclaimed 'twelve o'clock!' Whereupon we all rushed to the cloak-room – and *there* and in the lobby and up to the last moment the mirth raged on – Dickens took home Thackeray and Forster with him and his wife '*to finish the night there*' and a *royal* night they would have of it I fancy! – ending perhaps with a visit to the watch-house.

After all – the pleasantest company, as Burns thought, *are* the *blackguards!* – that is; those who have just a sufficient dash of blackguardism in them to make them snap their fingers at *ceremony* and 'all that sort of thing.' I question if there was as much witty speech uttered in all the aristocratic, conventional drawing rooms thro'out London that night as among us little knot of blackguardist literary people who felt ourselves above all rules, and independent of the universe! Well, and the result? Why the result my dear was, that I went to bed on my return and – slept like a top!!!!

Kate Cruise O'Brien
(1948–)

Kate Cruise O'Brien is the author of the short-story collection *A Gift Horse*, which won the Rooney Prize. She also edited *If Only, Short Stories of Love and Divorce* by Irish women writers, in 1997, to mark the introduction of divorce in Ireland. She is a columnist with the *Irish Independent* and lives in Dublin.

This extract comes from her novel *The Homesick Garden*, published in 1991. Antonia, the young heroine of the story, finds herself caught up in the domestic drama of some family friends when a needy stranger arrives on the doorstep on Christmas Eve.

On Christmas Eve the sky fell in. Mum was in the kitchen cooking. On Christmas Eve Mum boils the spiced beef. She rolls out the Jus-Rol puffed pastry and makes mince pies.

'Homemade, how are you,' she snarls. 'I make better pastry than his mother ever did because I use Jus-Rol. They could try that in an ad. They could also tell you that it's slavishness that counts at Christmas. It's not the pastry. It's the pain. I hate pastry and flour and rolling-pins but they haven't invented a mince pie that can be homemade without them. Yuch!' And Mum, being Mum, sprays flour all over the kitchen floor. On the other hand Mum tunes in to the Christmas carols on the radio. I've seen her cry into the flour when the solo boy soprano starts with 'Once in Royal David's City.' Mum sings along in her thready little voice, worn out with too much smoking.

Anyway this Christmas Eve, Mum was baking and boiling and crying and having, as far as I could tell, a perfectly splendid time, when the bell rang.

'Antonia!' roared Mum.

I was up watching television. There isn't room for anybody else in the kitchen when Mum starts on her Christmas Eve stint. And Mum won't have television in the kitchen. She says that the radio leaves her hands free but I think she wants would-be TV watchers out of her way. She does a lot of dreaming, does Mum with her radio. You can just see her making pictures in her head. But she doesn't like being interrupted so she's installed this ship's bell in the hall which she clangs if anyone has the nerve to ring the front doorbell. *I'm* supposed to answer the front door when I hear the ship's bell. It clanged. I opened the front door. There was this little blonde woman standing on the step. She was crying. She was thin, very thin and wearing a fur coat. A fur coat! Think of all the poor animals. Actually I rarely do. I mean I eat meat and walk on leather, for heaven's sake. But there was something terrible and pathetic about this little lady standing in our porch wearing fur when that's simply not done anymore and obviously she didn't know it. And her tears were making white tracks down her poor, thin, over-made-up face.

'Come in,' I said.

'I don't want to bother you. It's a bad time to come, Christmas Eve. Is your Mum in?'

She wasn't Dad's blonde. That was clear. She was blonde all right but her voice was Australian, and not confident Australian like you hear on *Neighbours*. It had a whining cringe to it. Dad likes women who stand up to him. Also he's a snob. He'd never go for an over-made-up peroxide blonde with the wrong sort of accent This woman looked like someone Mum would like because obviously she had problems. Mum isn't ever snobbish about problems or about anything else.

'Mum's in,' I said. 'She's crying in the kitchen.' I dragged the woman in. 'Mum's crying because it's Christmas and she always gets het up about Mary and the manger.' I was gabbing and rushing because, suddenly, I knew who this woman must be. This was Brian's wife. As Mum would say, who else could it be?

'Mum,' I said as I opened the kitchen door, 'Mum, this is a woman who wants to see you.'

Mum was red-eyed and flour-spattered. 'Oh,' she said.

'I said to your daughter I didn't want to bother you,' said the woman in a quick, fussy voice. 'I know it's Christmas and I'm sorta desperate. I came to spend Christmas here with my husband and he isn't *here*!'

And then she sat down at the kitchen table and started sobbing as if her heart would break.

'Oh dear, oh dear,' said Mum rushing across and patting the woman's fur shoulders with her floury hands. 'Oh dear. Husbands rarely are where they're supposed to be, particularly on Christmas Eve,' she said with a baleful look at the clock. Dad had been working lunch at the hotel this Christmas Eve. He should have been back hours, well one hour, ago.

'Who is your husband?' asked Mum. 'And why should he be here?'

'Not here in this house,' said the woman, sounding irritated. 'Here in *Dublin*. I went to his hotel. He wasn't there. He said he would be there but he wasn't. He told me about your family in his letters. He said you'd been 'A home from home.' He doesn't like home so I suppose there's a woman about. He thought the home business would make me feel better. It didn't, you know. The more lies he tells the more details he gives. The details are always OK. He has no imagination,' she said as if that made it worse. 'But the story is always wrong. The story is never true.'

'Did you come from Australia?' I asked. 'All that way?'

'No I did *not*! Did he tell you that? I did not. I'm a British citizen. I live in Birmingham. With him. Well I sometimes live with him. I did come from Australia. Brisbane as-a-matter-of-fact.' She said it all in one gulp. 'I wish I'd stayed there.'

'Well you can always go back if you want to,' said Mum calmly. I could see that she was thinking about kangaroos and flying doctors. She's always loved the thought of Australia. 'All that space,' she says dreamily as if she could see the tiny figures of Dad and me diminishing on a fading skyline.

'But you must tell me who you are?'

'You mean you don't know?' It seems snobbish to tell it the way she said it, 'You mean yu don't naow?'

'No,' said mum. 'I don't.'

'You let a perfect stranger in out of the night to cry on your Christmas table and you don't know!' (I can't do the naow bit again.) 'You don't know! Your daughter knows. All that talk of Australia. *She* knows.'

'You're Brian's wife,' I said . . .

'I'm Brian's wife,' said Marie. 'But what I want to know is where Brian is and what sort of story did he tell you?'

At this point there was the sound of a mighty rushing wind, which meant someone had opened the front door. There was a crash (door slamming) and a stumble.

'I'm drunk!' carolled Dad from the hall. 'I'm very very drunk. I've been drinking and drinking and drinking since lunch time and now I'd like to pinch a fat lady's bottom. Where is my wife, my moderately fat wife? Not that her bottom is fat. It's just her middle.'

'Do you have to put up with that all the time?' said Marie, sounding awed.

'Not often,' said Mum who'd got the giggles. 'Not half often enough. I'm the one who drinks around here. He only gets festive once every decade. I think he must have taken to the

Leeson Street strip and got involved with too many Tequila Sunrises. He's a very innocent drinker. He thinks sweet is safe. Don't mind him. He's quite harmless.'

'Oh-my-God!' said Marie.

It was six o'clock on Christmas morning. There was a truly horrid sound from upstairs. Dad was being sick. Mum had left him a bucket so it was none of my business anyway. I flipped up the blind and looked out. It was still and quiet and peaceful. Just a few lights on in the road. Perhaps there were children rustling around the Christmas trees. I felt suddenly homesick for the way it had been. Stockings and stars and excitement in the morning. Aunt Grace coming at eleven, with, always, the most magic present of all. I wandered into the dining-room to look at the tree. This was my time in the house. The time when I owned it. There, under the tree, was the most enormous big box, a big crude cardboard box covered with ivy, the blackened sort which grew on the wall outside the dining-room. The ivy had been sprayed silver over the black and there was this notice on the front: FOR ANTONIA FROM SANTA. It's not when people are nasty to you that you want to cry. It's often when they're suddenly, unexpectedly, nice.

Santa had left a lot of presents for Antonia. Sweets and oranges, books, the best sort. Mum is very good at books. No scarves, which I hate, but two of those games which bubble and tumble in plastic before your eyes. From Dad, I guessed. And two tapes. Not Strauss waltzes or Beethoven, the only kind of classical music Mum can stand. Early Christian music, breathing prayer, the kind that Dad likes and I like which is

odd since we're both much less naturally religious than Mum
is. I mean none of us believes in God but Mum still lights candles in darkened churches and thinks it will work. 'You weren't
even reared a Catholic,' says Dad, who was. 'That's why,' says
Mum. At the bottom of the box there was this other little box.
A black, velvet, rectangular box. On the top of the box there
was a kind of cat's cradle of sticky-tape, grimy sticky tape,
enclosing a white envelope. Fairly white. Mum never could
manage parcels. Inside was a card:

Dear Antonia,
   When I was fifteen my godmother gave me these pearls.
   I'm handing them on to you because I love you. I know, I
   know you'd hate me to mention it but I do anyway.
      Much love, Elizabeth . . . Your Mother.

Emily Dickinson
(1830–96)

Emily Dickinson was born in Amherst, Massachusetts and except for a brief spell in Boston, spent her whole life in the family home there. She was popular as a young girl and had a close circle of friends, but from around 1862 she cut herself off from most of her friends and refused to see visitors, earning herself the sobriquet 'the Myth of Amherst'. Although she was an extremely prolific poet, writing nearly two thousand poems, only seven were published during her lifetime. Her work is intensely personal and spiritual. She is considered by some to be the inventor of modern American poetry, although she was barely understood or appreciated during her lifetime.

In this letter to her friend Abiah Root, written while still in her teens, Emily describes the Christmas festivities of 1845 and reveals her dark state of mind at the start of the new year. Despite the gloom, Dickinson's whimsical humour reasserts itself in the end.

12 January 1846

Abiah, my dear,

Since I received your precious letter another year has commenced its course, and the old year has gone never to return. How sad it makes one feel to sit down quietly and think of the flight of the old year, and the unceremonious obtrusion of the new year upon our notice! How many things we have omitted to do which might have cheered a human heart, or whispered hope in the ear of the sorrowful, and how many things have we done over which the dark mantle of regret will ever fall! How many good resolutions did I make at the commencement of the year now flown, merely to break them and to feel more than ever convinced of the weakness of my own resolutions! The New Year's day was unusually gloomy to me, I know not why, and perhaps for that reason a host of unpleasant reflections forced themselves upon me which I found not easy to throw off. But I will no longer sentimentalize upon the past, for I cannot recall it. I will, after inquiring for the health of my dear Abiah, relapse into a more lively strain . . .

I suppose from your letter that you are enjoying yourself finely this winter at Miss Campbell's school. I would give a great deal if I was there with you. I don't go to school this winter except to a recitation in German. Mr C[oleman] has a very large class, and father thought I might never have another opportunity to study it. It takes about an hour and a half to recite. Then I take music lessons and practise two hours a day, and besides these two I have a large stand of plants to cultivate. This is the principal round of my occupation this winter . . . I have just seen a funeral procession go by of a negro baby, so if my ideas are rather dark you need not marvel ... Old Santa Claus was very polite to me the last Christmas. I hung up my stocking on the bedpost as usual. I had a perfume bag and a bottle of otto of rose to go with it, a sheet of music, a china mug with *Forget me not* upon it, from. S. S., – who, by the way, is as handsome, entertaining, and as fine a piano player as in former times, – a toilet cushion, a watch case, a fortune-teller, and an amaranthine stock of pin-cushions and needlebooks, which in ingenuity and art would rival the works of Scripture Dorcas. I found abundance of candy in my stocking, which I do not think has had the anticipated effect upon my disposition, in case it was to sweeten it, also two hearts at the bottom of all, which I thought looked rather ominous; but I will not enter into any more details, for they take up more room than I can spare.

Haven't we had delightful weather for a week or two? It seems as if Old Winter had forgotten himself. Don't you believe he is absentminded? It has been bad weather for colds, however. I have had a severe cold for a few days, and can sympathize with you, though I have been delivered from a stiff neck. I think you must belong to the tribe of Israel, for you know in the Bible the prophet calls them a stiff-necked generation. I have lately come to the conclusion that I am Eve, alias Mrs Adam. You know there is no account of her death in the Bible, and why am not I Eve? If you find any statements which you think likely to prove the truth of the case, I wish you would send them to me without delay ...

Virginia Woolf
(1882–1941)

Virginia Woolf was born in London, the daughter of the publisher Sir Leslie Stephen. From an early age, she entertained her family with her stories. When her father died in 1904, the family moved to Bloomsbury where they formed the core of the Bloomsbury Group of philosophers, writers and artists. With her husband, Leonard Woolf, whom she married in 1912, she founded the Hogarth Press. Virginia Woolf's works include several volumes of letters, diaries and essays, but she is best known for her experimental novels such as *To the Lighthouse* (1927) and *The Waves* (1931) and she is considered one of the great innovators of the genre. Although she was a prolific and successful writer, and her private correspondence shows an irrepressible wit and humour, she was beset with recurring depression and debilitating headaches. She finally drowned herself in 1941 in the River Ouse near her home in Sussex.

These two extracts are from Christmas letters written to the French artist Jacques Raverat and to her dear friend and sometime lover, Vita Sackville-West.

Monk's House, Rodmell,
[Sussex]
Dec. 26th 1924

My dear Jacques,

Do not expect wit or sense in this letter, only the affection of a drugged and torpid mind. Oh an English Christmas! We are not Christians; we are not social; we have no part in the fabric of the world, but all the same, Christmas flattens us out like a steam roller; turkey, pudding, tips, waits, holly, good wishes, presents, sweets; so here we sit, on Boxing day, at Rodmell, over a wood fire, and I can only rouse myself by thinking of you. In particular, I want to know 1. how you are. 2. Whether you are getting on with your autobiography; 3. What you are thinking; 4. what feeling; 5. what imagining, criticising, seeing – do catch that wild woman Gwen* and stick a pen in her paw.

Monk's House, Rodmell,
Lewes, [Sussex]
Dec. 26th 1924

My dear Vita,

It is sad that you should be determined to undermine my virtue.[†] Never have I been so happy as I was two nights ago, though we had the dullest possible party. (a purely business conversation) Still I sipped my glass, I became more and more

---

*   Gwen Darwin, Raverat's wife. The couple lived at Vence, near Nice.
†   Vita had given Virginia a bottle of Spanish wine as a Christmas present.

genial, more and more condescending, affable and intimate, till the company was suspicious. But really you ought to keep these treats for my visits to you. Home tippling will be my ruin.

We are badly in want of a drop here, in this watery and tee-total house, where the turkey and cold sausages are never finished.

We are sitting over the fire – at 6 o'clock on Xmas Eve, as we were packing to come here, arrived an order from America for 25 Seducers.* Off we went to the post in the rain – then I had a sip to warm me. 899 Seducers sold.

A thousand thanks for the bottle – and please come and see us again soon –

Yr V.W.

I hope you are better.

---

*   *Seducers in Ecuador*, Sackville-West's novel.

christmas abroad

Around the hotel pool Christmas trees
And flame hibiscus glow with fairy lights.
Carols, songs from Bollywood.

VALERIE JOSEPHS

Rose Macaulay
(1881–1958)

Rose Macaulay was an English novelist, travel writer, literary critic and poet. She spent part of her childhood in Italy, due to her mother's poor health, and this period gave rise to her life-long interest in travel. She set several of her books, including *The Towers of Trebizond* (1956), in Mediterranean countries. She returned to England when she was in her teens, and, after graduating from Somerville College, Oxford with a degree in history, she wrote her first novel, *The Valley of Captives* (1911). The satirical novels that followed, such as *Potterism* (1920) and *Told by an Idiot* (1923), poked fun at British manners and politics and were hugely successful.

Macaulay worked as a columnist at the *Spectator* for many years and the extract below, 'Saturnalia', was first published in the November 1957 issue. It describes her Christmases in Italy, many years before, where her family was the only one to observe the beloved English customs. Her tone changes as she moves to the present, describing what she views as the iniquities of modern Christmas.

When I was a child, many years ago, in a then still almost medieval Italian town, no one but we decorated houses with holly or mistletoe, and ours was the only Christmas tree; we invited our neighbours to see it, and they were overwhelmed with delighted amaze at the candled tree with its angels and coloured glass ornaments. *'Che bel costume!'* they cried; and they liked too the holly over the pictures, but never, I think, adopted either custom themselves. Nor did we ever see Christmas mummers, and eating and drinking was in moderation, and Christmas presents were not exchanged, nor cards, and no one sang carols in the streets. The twelve days of Christmas passed quietly, and even Twelfth Day was not uproarious. The churches were not decorated either, but they all had a *presepio*, and the figures for these were sold everywhere; we assembled our own, adding sheep, cows, shepherds, magi, as could afford them, and once we got a very fine camel. We felt pity for the Italian children, because they had no Christmas stockings, no presents, no tree. We came to regard Christmas as an English feast, which foreigners did not understand, and when we went to live in England and saw the Christmas junketings, the carolling, the carousings, the mummers coming round, the churches gay with the Ivy and the holly, the Twelfth Night revels, we felt that we had come into our national heritage, disgusting though the weather was.

But we were young. We did not know the grim toil that our saturnalia even then involved for our elders. Nor could we guess that it would swell with the years until it became the monstrous expenditure of time, money, strength, health and temper that now it is. Chaos in the streets, madness in the shops, hard labour in the house, expensive toys ill-afforded, expensive food gorged, while in desolate camps far off those driven from their homes shiver and starve. A good time is not had by all, cannot, for lack of means, be had by most. But our rich saturnalia romps along; the churches are crowded for midnight Mass; de luxe Cribs glitter with candles and stars, and the magi ride in with their expensive gifts, while the incense-swinging procession winds round the church, and we sing '*Adeste Fideles*', and the herald angels sing improbably of peace on earth; how in the world did they think of that?

We go home from church to bed, and wake to more presents, more fun. By and large, the wrong people get the presents and the fun, the people who had plenty of presents and fun before.

Valerie Josephs
(contemporary)

Valerie Josephs lives in London, where she was born. She has also spent time in Paris, Chicago and Glasgow. She trained as a sculptor at The Art Institute of Chicago and the Central St Martins School of Art in London, and later studied Fine Art Photography at Glasgow School of Art. She has a Masters degree in Art and Architecture from the University of Kent. Her artworks, sometimes using text, have been exhibited in England and abroad. In 1989 she won an award to photograph in Japan. Since starting to write in 1994, travel has been a recurring theme in Josephs' work, as in this poem, 'Christmas in Cochin'. Her poems have appeared in *Still, Journal of London Independent Photography* and *Poetry Street*.

Vasco da Gama came here for pepper.
His grave is in St Francis Church where the British
left punkahs pulled by ropes to make a breeze.
Chinese nets from the court of Kublai Khan
need four fishermen to raise the weights and levers.
In the raja's palace there are scenes
from the Ramayana painted on the walls.
Around the hotel pool Christmas trees
and flame hibiscus glow with fairy lights.
Carols, songs from Bollywood.
I walk along Jew Town Road in blazing sun
past the spice market: cinnamon, cardamom and star-
    anise,
to the synagogue built on land the raja gave the
    Jews –
the Portuguese were burning them at the stake.
Now five families remain to protect the scrolls.
In Mr Radhakrishnan's Kathakali
performers paint their faces in vermilion, green and
    white;
black soot for beards and eyes and brows.
Hands speak of sun rising, mountains, door of a
    house
and bees sucking honey from a lotus flower.

Dame Freya Stark
(1893–1993)

Dame Freya Stark was born in Paris but spent her childhood in England and Italy. She was a nurse on the Italian front during World War I and afterwards studied Arabic at the School of Oriental and African studies at the University of London. She travelled extensively, especially in the Middle East, and wrote more than 30 books about her experiences, including *The Southern Gates of Arabia* (1936) and *Beyond Euphrates* (1951). Her correspondence, often with her mother, Flora, reveals more of the personal side of her epic journeys.

This letter to Flora Stark describes a Christmas spent in Aden in 1934. In characteristic fashion Stark shuns the formal party and takes off on a risky boat trip with the father of a friend.

26 December 1934

Darling B.,

Christmas day is over. Poor Meryem had all the staff to dinner – twenty-two people, including me. She rather likes a little indiscriminate gaiety, poor child, and hardly ever indulges in it. 'Elle est superficielle d'une façon étonnante,' says M. Besse, while she struggles over his cablegrams, and he says no to all the parties: he adores her with complete possessiveness which is bound to lead to trouble. They were working all day yesterday, and this dinner party loomed larger and larger as the afternoon drew on. 'Je ne le supporterai pas,' said M. Besse: 'you and I will leave them; we will go in the launch on the sea.' I made a feeble effort to stand by Meryem, who had sixteen men and only four ladies: she however said that it was well worth while to get rid of her father, who would cast gloom over all the young clerks' efforts at cheerfulness.

After tea he took me out for a drive to the mainland – Sheikh Othman – where the sea character of Aden changes to desert filled with little bushes and coloured pebbles. It was a lovely sunset, in a sky so golden that the disk of the sun itself could not be seen – it was all one molten colour. He comes riding here with his wife when she is here: she must be a rather charming woman by what he says of her. We came back in a more peaceful frame of mind, but at a pace which penetrated even to my ignorance: I looked at the speedometer and saw it just touching fifty miles an hour. M. Besse relapsed into gloom as the hour drew near: I found him all ready dressed like a sac- rificial victim and a lovely table laid on the roof: all the young clerks, very shy and naturally not a bit at their best. We played consequences and read them out – pulled crackers – and then when they started to dance M. Besse murmured that 'Je ne le supporte plus: est-ce que vous venez?' He vanished and got into white clothes: seized an armful of coats for me, opened a trap door down the back stairs, and crept out to the car, leaving the party to its fate. Herbert will sympathise. We motored down to the port; found the launch and Somali chauffeur waiting with the rising moon, and were off with a most delightful feeling of escapade. It was such fun. We passed by all the lights of Aden – people dancing in bungalows, sailors feasting on the ships: we made for the entrance point; and sea and wind freshened, we were round the corner under the black hills and rocks, Orion above, and Taurus and the Pleiades. Then no lights at all, except three yellow and a green from some travelling ship at sea: the spray in a light rain on our faces: M. Besse and I lying in great comfort on cushions, while he kept the tiller with one hand – the Somali, with his big turban sticking up in a little tuft, looking out to sea ahead of us. 'On se lave l'âme,' said M. Besse, and made a little gesture of horror every time I mentioned the party. We went on and on. 'I know a cave, we could sleep on the sand,' said M. Besse, 'but Meryem would be anxious.' I thought this quite as well, as I may just as well keep some shred of reputation while I am about it. But we still went on – the sea getting more of a swell while M. Besse told me how he and his wife had just saved their lives round this corner. We saw a sort of halo round a bend, and suddenly opened a long spit of land and a little solitary lighthouse as black as the rocks it stood on: it was a peculiar lighthouse, worked by a black shutter which went down over its light and up again instead of a circular movement: the effect was indescribably malignant, as if a hooded figure were masking and unmasking itself, a kind of Moloch idol waiting for victims: the spit of rock came down like a snout with a hole like an eye through which the sky shone: the moon hid behind clouds; the water boiled round the headland, several currents meeting: and the clockwork regularity of that malevolent black figure of the lighthouse gave an eeriness quite inexpressible. 'This corner is what we always call the *chaudron*, because the water bubbles up,' said M. Besse. 'It is very difficult to steer. I used to like to hold my life by a thread, but now I do not think it right to do so any longer' – and we were tossed about by a broadside wave like a coracle. 'I do not like the way our motor works,' he chose this moment to say.

We were tossed from side to side, the waves heaved their backs all round us, I had not the faintest idea where we were, what time or what world we were in. We made for a cleft between the mainland and an island; shot through with great skill; saw a little sleeping beach and tall houses. I couldn't think where we were. M. Besse refused to say: he suggested it might be the moon: he went through some tortuous little ways by a small white mosque, by a few sleeping goats who looked familiar, and landed at his own door: we had come right round the Aden volcano, which is attached to the land by only a very narrow neck. I don't believe I have ever enjoyed a Christmas evening quite so much.

    Your own

    Freya

Lady Mary Anne Barker
(later Lady Broome)
(1831–1911)

Lady Mary Anne Barker was born in Jamaica, the daughter of
the Colonial Secretary. Her second husband, Sir Frederick
Napier Broome, was Governor of Trinidad. She wrote a number
of books about life in far outposts of the British Empire, including *Station Life in New Zealand* (1870), *A Year's Housekeeping in
South Africa* (1877) and *Colonial Memories* (1904). In this tale,
from *A Christmas Cake in Four Quarters* (1871), the inveterate
storyteller Mrs Owen describes a comical Christmas feast in
Jamaica.

'Then, as if we had not laughing enough before dinner, we had a dreadful trial of our gravity during that meal. The party was rather a large one, for our father always made it a rule to invite new comers, or people who had no family circle of their own, to dine with us on that day, declaring that he had spent *one* solitary Christmas in his life, and had found it so inexpressibly dreary and sad, that he could not bear to think of anyone else doing so. Now the great difficulty at these Christmas festivities was *the* plum-pudding. Very few negro cooks (they are all men by the way) had the remotest idea of what a plum-pudding was like, for it is by no means a favourite dish in the tropics. Indeed no one ever thought of having such a rich, hot thing except at Christmas; and in the generality of tropical households, after many efforts and many failures, it had at last been given up. Mamma would have rejoiced at the abandonment of the national dish, for she had gone through severe trials connected with it; but Papa considered it a dreadful, almost a wicked thing, to sit down to dinner on Christmas Day without roast beef, turkey, mince-pies, *and* a plum-pudding. So, instead of our usual nice, light, digestible dinner, suited to the climate, we found ourselves a large party, sitting round our Christmas dinner table laden with English fare. Poor Mamma had two great anxieties on her mind. There was the uncertainty when and how the pudding might make its appearance. Once it had been sent up in the form of sauce, to be handed about with the mince-pies; and on other occasions it had come to table tied up in its cloth, and the whole affair had been set on fire by the butler, who thought it was all right, and poured the blazing brandy over it before he could be prevented. Her second great dread was that any of the guests should mention or allude to Cousin Paul. There was nothing Papa disliked so much as giggling; and if Paul's name had been uttered, it is quite certain that Frances and I would have behaved badly in that respect. My own belief is that Mamma went about before dinner entreating her guests not to mention Paul's name, for the way the subject was avoided struck us afterwards as being very suspicious.

'However, all went well until it was time for the second course to appear. Everything had been removed belonging to the first course, and servant after servant went out of the room to see what had become of the sweet things. Mamma grew paler and more nervous at each moment's delay, and murmured plaintively to her neighbour, 'I am sure it is the plum-pudding.' But it was *not* the pudding – at least no pudding appeared; and at last my father said sternly to the butler, who alone remained in the room, –

'"We can't wait all night for the pudding, James; send it in just as it is; or let us have the rest of the dinner, at all events."

'James bowed gravely and departed; a moment after he left the dining-room we heard a wild scuffling and confusion outside and many "Hi's" – "'top him." In rushed the black cook, Alphonse by name, very tipsy, with his shirt sleeves rolled up, his cooking apron fluttering behind him, and bearing in his outstretched arms a very large dish, which he set down before Mamma, crying, –

'"Dere, my good Missus, dere your puddin's; Alphonse make dem fuss-class. James say dem too small. Cho! him know noting 'bout puddin'. 'Top one littel minnit, Alphonse break him sarcy head;" and out he dashed to carry his threat into execution.

'Certainly the puddings were small, very small; in fact they were no bigger than Violet's little fist. Three or four of the diminutive dainties, looking exactly like tiny cannon-balls, reposed, with wide spaces between each, on the huge dish. Mamma gazed mournfully at them and said, "I wonder why he has boiled it in separate pieces like this." Papa took a more cheerful view of matters and cried gaily, "Never mind, mother, I daresay they taste very good; let us each have a little bit, – just for luck, you know." Mamma shook her head, for she had grave misgivings about their taste, but she took up a spoon and attempted to carry out her husband's directions. We all watched her in breathless silence. First she tried one small pudding and then another – tried to help it, I mean – but the moment she touched it with a spoon, the hard little lump bounced away. It was impossible to catch it, and, after chasing the refractory hard lumps of pudding round the dish, she laid down the spoon in despair.

'"Let me try," said the gentleman nearest to her, and he seized a spoon with more goodwill than judgment, for the moment he tried to get the pudding into a corner of the dish, and divide it into two pieces, it sprang bodily out of the dish and leapt, like an india-rubber ball, right into the lap of one of the guests.

'"It is as hard as a stone," said its new possessor. "I don't believe I could cut it with a knife;" and as he spoke he tried to hold it with his fork and cut it with his knife. But he was equally unsuccessful: the pudding slipped as skilfully way from under the sharp blade as it had done from the spoon, and bounded off to the opposite side of the table.

'I remember quite well that we let the other puddings alone: they appeared to be all equally solid and equally averse to being eaten; so James once more took up the first of this strange species of Christmas fare, and putting it back on the dish, carried the whole affair off to Alphonse, who had been tied into his chair, and who was so enraged at the rejection of his cherished dainties that he shied them one after the other at the butler's retreating figure. Certainly James made a most undignified and hasty entrance into the dining-room, and we heard a sound as of a stone following him closely.

'"Is that a plum-pudding, James?" asked my father.'

Lady Mary Wortley Montagu
(1689–1762)

Lady Mary was a great figure of the eighteenth century. She was a prolific and witty letter-writer, poet, traveller, and society hostess numbering Swift, Addison and Pope among her friends. However, she had a celebrated quarrel with the latter, arising out of her satirical *Town Eclogues*, published in 1716. In 1712 she married Edward Wortley Montagu against the wishes of her family, and on his appointment as Ambassador to Constantinople, accompanied him to Turkey. She recorded her impressions of the East in her vivid letters home. While in Turkey, she became acquainted with the practice of inoculation against smallpox and was instrumental in the introduction of the vaccination in Britain. In 1737 she left her husband and country and settled in Italy, only returning home on the death of Sir Edward in 1761. Lady Bute, her only daughter, was married to John Stuart Bute, who was Prime Minister from 1762 until 1763.

In this letter to her daughter, dated January 5th, 1748, she describes Christmas festivities at Gottolengo, Brescia, where she was living under the protection of her friend Count Palazzi.

Dear Child,

... I had a visit in the beginning of these holidays of thirty horse of ladies and gentlemen with their servants (by the way, the ladies all ride like the late Duchess of Cleveland). They came with the kind intent of staying with me at least a fortnight, though I had never seen any of them before; but they were all neighbours within ten mile round. I could not avoid entertaining them at supper, and by good luck had a large quantity of game in the house, which with the help of my poultry furnished out a plentiful table. I sent for the fiddles; and they were so obliging to dance all night, and even dine with me next day, though none of them had been in bed, and were much disappointed I did not press them to stay, it being the fashion to go in troops to one another's houses, hunting and dancing together, a month in each castle. I have not yet returned any of their visits, nor do not intend it of some time, to avoid this expensive hospitality. The trouble of it is not very great, they not expecting any ceremony. I left the room about one o'clock, and they continued their ball in the salon above stairs without being at all offended by my departure. The greatest diversion I had was to see a lady of my own age comfortably dancing with her own husband some years older, and I can assure you she jumps and gallops with the best of them.

the real gifts: christmas transformations

Heavens, the joy was truly terrifying.

ISABEL BOLTON

Elizabeth Goudge
(1900–84)

Elizabeth Goudge was a prolific writer of novels, short stories, plays and children's books. She was also an artist and a teacher of handicrafts, such as weaving and embroidery. Her accurate portraits of English life in small towns gave her work great popular appeal. Her best-known tale, *Green Dolphin Country*, written during World War II, won the Metro-Goldwyn-Mayer Literary Award in 1944 and was filmed in 1947 as *Green Dolphin Street*.

The extract here is from her novel *Towers in the Mist*, published in 1938. In it, Goudge conjures up all the boisterousness and cosiness of an unselfconsciously joyful English Christmas, and does so with a relish for detail that is reminiscent of Dickens.

As the month drew on the thought of the stars was in every-one's minds, for Christmas was coming in in the traditional way, with frost and snow upon the ground and such a blaze of constellations in the night sky that it seemed the heavens were hanging low over the earth in most unusual friendliness.

And certainly the city of Oxford was good to look at at this time. By day, under a brilliant blue sky, the gabled roofs and tall chimneys, the towers and spires, took on an added bright-ness from the tracery of sparkling frost that clung to them; and down below them the narrow streets were bright with the bunchy little figures of snowballing children, happy girls and beaming mothers going shopping with baskets on their arms, dressed in their gaudiest because it was Christmas-time, and laughing men with sprigs of holly in their caps, and faces as rosy as apples from the potations they had partaken of at the taverns and inns in honour of the festive season. The bad smells of the town had been obliterated by the continual snow showers and the hard frost – it would be a different story when the thaw came, but sufficient unto the day is the evil thereof – and delicious festive scents floated out into the streets from open doors and windows; scents of baked meats and roasting apples, of ale and wine, of spices and perfumes and the fra-grant wood-smoke from innumerable fires of apple-wood and beech-logs and resinous pine-branches. And at night the city seemed almost as brilliant as the starry sky above. From sheer goodwill doors were left ajar and windows uncurtained, so that bright beams of light lay aslant across the shadows, and the gay groups that thronged the streets carried lanterns that bobbed like fireflies over the trampled snow. The bells rang out continuously and the laughter and clear voices of the children made unceasing music . . . And outside the city walls the fields and the low hills lay silent, shrouded in white. The murmur of the streams was hushed by the ice and the willow trees drooped above them without movement.

II

On Christmas Eve, after the sun had set, it all seemed a little intensified; the stars shone yet more brilliantly, the bells rang clearer and sweeter, the firelight seemed ruddier and the laugher and gaiety of the townspeople more contagious. Yet Nicolas, as he strolled idly across Carfax into Cornmarket, felt oddly apart from it all. Used as he was to being always at the centre of whatever excitement was afoot this unusual loneliness was a little frightening. It was because he was so unhappy, he thought, that he felt so lonely. It seemed that suffering of any sort made one feel lonely. He had not suffered before and so he had not discovered this before. He wondered why it should be so, for one was not alone in suffering; the whole world suffered. Perhaps this loneliness had some purpose in the scheme of things . . .

Bands of travelling players still journeyed up and down the country, playing the old Morality Plays in the inn yards and at the market crosses, and their coming was still one of the events of the year at Oxford . . .

The rough wooden stage was set up in the middle of the courtyard, as though at the heart of the world, lighted at each

corner by lanterns and decked with holly and evergreens, with
the gaily dressed trumpeter standing upon it with his trumpet
to his lips; and all round it surged the jolly Christmas crowd,
fighting to get up to the best seats in the gallery that ran round
the courtyard, or failing that, a place on the wooden steps that
led up to it, or failing that an inch of room in the packed space
below. Aldermen and citizens with their fat wives and rosy
children were there, apprentices and pretty girls, rogues and
vagabonds and dirty little urchins, all pushing and kicking and
scrambling, but brimming over with humour and goodwill.
They knew how to enjoy themselves on Christmas Eve, did
these people of Oxford, and they were doing it . . .

They were playing an old Nativity play to-night, followed by
the story of Saint Nicolas, and he was no sooner in his place,
then the trumpeter stepped down, the lights in the gallery were
hidden, and in a sudden silence, that fell upon the noisy crowd
as though the shadow of an angel's wing passed over them, the
first figures of the Christmas story stepped upon the stage.

It was very crude and at some other time Nicolas might have
been moved to mirth, but he was not so moved to-night, neither he nor a single man, woman or child in that densely
packed throng. It was Christmas Eve, and the same stars shone
above them as had shone upon the fields of Palestine some fifteen hundred years ago. They sat in a deep and lovely silence,
their eyes riveted upon the rough wooden stage where the figures of shepherds moved, and angels whose dresses had shrunk
in the wash and whose wings and haloes had become a little
battered by so much packing and unpacking, and a Virgin Mary
whose blue cloak was torn and whose voice was that of a young

English peasant boy who had not so long ago been taken from the plough.

Wedged against the balustrade of the gallery, Nicolas watched and listened in that state of heavenly concentration that leaves the human creature oblivious of himself. He was not conscious any more of the apprentices who pressed upon him, or of the smell of unwashed human bodies, or of his own empty stomach that had been presented with no supper this evening. He was only dimly aware of the crowd as a great multitude that he could not number, watchers in the shadows who had been watching there for fifteen hundred years. The Christmas story itself absorbed him. Though it was so old a story, one that he had known as soon as he was capable of knowing anything, it seemed to-night quite new to him. 'Glory to God in the highest . . . A child is born.' The old words that he had heard a hundred times over seemed cried out with the triumph of new and startling news. The figures that moved before him, Mary with the child in her arms, Joseph and the shepherds, Gabriel and the angels, Herod and the Wise Men, that he had seen so many times pictured in stained-glassed windows and on the leaves of missals, moved now in this tiny space at the heart of the crowd as though they had come there for the first time . . . The love of God is with man . . . That, Nicolas knew suddenly, is the news of the far country, the mystery like a nugget of gold that men travel so far to seek, the fact that is stated but not explained by all the pictures that have been painted and by all the music and the poetry that has been written since the dawn of the world. It was as easy as that, and as difficult.

Christina Rossetti
(1830–94)

Christina Rossetti was born in London, the daughter of Gabriele Rossetti and sister of Dante Gabriel Rossetti. She was educated at home and her first books of poetry were printed when she was still in her teens. She was also an artist and a children's writer and, after her father retired from his post as Professor of Italian at the University of London, she supplemented her family's income by teaching Italian and writing. Rossetti was a devout Christian and for some time carried out charity work at a refuge for single mothers and prostitutes in Highgate. She was plagued by ill health and became increasingly infirm after she developed Graves Disease. Her preoccupation with death is manifest in many of her later poems.

Rossetti is one of England's most important nineteenth-century women poets. Her Christmas carols and hymns are universally loved. Less well known is this untitled poem, describing the poet's tender feelings as she watches her mother sleeping in her chair on Christmas Day, 1882.

My blessed Mother dozing in her chair
On Christmas Day seemed an embodied Love,
A comfortable Love with soft brown hair
Softened and silvered to a tint of dove;
A better sort of Venus with an air
Angelical from thoughts that dwell above;
A wiser Pallas in whose body fair
Enshrined a blessed soul looks out thereof.
Winter brought holly then; now Spring has brought
Paler and frailer snowdrops shivering;
And I have brought a simple humble thought –
I her devoted duteous Valentine –
A lifelong thought which thrills this song I sing,
A livelong love to this dear Saint of mine.

Mrs Patrick Campbell
(1865–1940)

Beatrice Stella Campbell was born in London of mixed Italian and English parentage. Her stage career began in 1888, and although her volatile temperament sometimes made her difficult to work with, she was extremely talented and successful. She played Eliza in George Bernard Shaw's *Pygmalion* and formed a long friendship with the playwright. He fell violently in love with her, pelted her with passionate letters and wrote plays for her. She gracefully evaded his romantic attentions and they managed to retain a friendship. This extract from her memoir *My Life and Some Letters* (1922) describes the unforgettable moment when one Christmas marked the end of carefree, boundary-free childhood and the beginning of real life.

I remember clearly my first grief. There was a children's party given by my father – a Christmas tree with a lovely fairy doll holding a golden sceptre in her hand, and with, what appeared to me, a diamond crown upon her head, standing on the tips of her toes, with stars all about her and lights – lights every-where – and toys of all descriptions and colours hanging everywhere beneath her feet.

At the foot of the tree were large crackers – bigger than I – and I was told that inside these crackers were dresses – kings' dresses, queens' dresses, princes' and princesses'. A band was playing. Crowds of people and children and I, wild with excitement, looking, wondering whether I would have the dress of a queen or a princess.

Then someone brought me one of the large crackers and said it was mine. I put my arms around it, and whispered: 'What is inside?' And the answer, I know, was 'A cook's dress', and I wept and wept and wept.

I remember no more about the Christmas party, only that I was in a room alone. Someone had grown tired of telling me to 'stop crying', 'not to be a silly little girl'. I was full of shame, and my vain little heart was broken.

Isabel Bolton (Mary Britton Miller)
(1883–1975)

Isabel Bolton was the author of several volumes of poetry and collections of verse for children published under her own name. Her first novel, *In the Days of Thy Youth*, appeared in 1943. She did not start writing novels under her pseudonym until she was in her sixties. As well as her novels, she wrote a memoir about the accidental death by drowning of her identical twin sister in *Under Gemini* (1967). Frequently classed with her compatriots, Edith Wharton and Henry James, she spent most of her life in and around the New York City she conjures so magically in her books.

This extract is from her 1949 novel, *The Christmas Tree*. Here, Bolton describes the power of the season and its symbols to evoke potent and picturesque memories in an elderly woman struggling to come to terms with the fractured family life of modern times.

The Christmas Season, thought Mrs Danforth, pacing up and down her living room, did queer things to you, compassing you round with all your memories – remembering other Christmases, you might indeed say other existences; for she was one to keep an eye on her own mortality, and the sum total of her experiences gave her frequently the oddest sense of having led many different lives and passed through many periods of history. Not only had she seen astonishing changes take place in the exterior, the material world, but what startling revolutions seemed to have occurred within men's souls – the gestures and gestations of the spirit, the morals and manners of today! Lord, if you allowed this accumulation of memories and impressions to play over you – if you returned to thinking of the days when you were young.

One waited, she remembered, her memories of Christmas beginning to dissolve into a sense of a far-distant past, and watching the fine small snowflakes whirled round the corner of her high balconies and terraces from one December to the next, and all the days between flavored with just a bit of Christmas expectation. There had been those fabulous practically legendary New York winters, the horse cars and the horse-drawn busses on the Avenue and frequently sleighs dashing through the Park in a bright scatter of snow and simultaneous sleigh bells – and the sound of wagon wheels and carriage wheels creaking in the cold, the plonk, plonk of the horses' hoofs – all the streets so very orderly and given over, to use that worn-out phrase, to 'people of one's own class,' the snow so very clean, piled neatly up on either side along the curb, lying along the area railings, and along the brownstone balustrades, with few buildings higher than the familiar church steeples on the Avenue, and coming as one did at Forty-second Street upon the reservoir surrounded by the high stone wall so sparsely grown with ivy, and all the sparrows twittering.

At this point in her perambulations, Mrs Danforth stopped a moment to take a look at her little grandson who was stretched out on the window seat completely absorbed in some game or other that apparently involved a piece of wood, a wire, and a bit of string, and deciding as she regarded him that she would give him this year a Christmas tree, she visualized it – there in the center of the room, lighted by real candles and resembling, if possible, the kind of tree she used to have when she was young.

Poor little Henry, she thought, resuming her walk, a rather mean time in many ways modern children seemed to have of it. No stability around them – hardly a bed to call their own – what with their cramped manner of living, dwelling in apartment houses and all . . .

When she compared her fidelity toward everything and everyone surrounding her, her utter trust in life, with Henry's complete lack of faith in any kind of security – for as far as she could see there was no safety for him anywhere, taking as he had completely for granted this change and that goodbye, the next reunion, adapting himself as best he could to whatever freakish novelty life might present to him, and hardly ever knowing what sort of bed he was likely to sleep in from one month to the next, and possessing, if she recollected correctly, neither aunts nor uncles to buttress up his faith in a toppling world – when she came to think of it all, which little soul had been the best prepared to meet the events in wait for it?

However unable she felt to answer the question, Henry should, she decided, have his Christmas tree. What might occur in the interval between then and now, or where the child was likely to be, whether sheltered by her, or by his mother and the Captain, or even, perhaps, claimed at the last moment by his father, it would not be her business to determine. But at least she could arrange this little celebration. She'd invite in a few people; she'd make it gay and festive. Henry should have his tree.

Not that children felt today the way that she had felt about Christmas in her childhood, for along with all the other changes, this change in the Christmas spirit she definitely believed had taken place. Though there was all manner of evidence of the season – New York producing it, as it produced everything else, on its own colossal, mass-production scale, all outdoors and public and promiscuous, with a tree in almost every park and square, all the churches turning them out properly lighted and arrayed, the great central civic spectacle there in Rockefeller Center, the tallest Christmas tree erected on this earth, standing up in all the majesty of its broad green boughs, with those beautiful balloons floating like celestial bodies of blue and gold and silver all around it, while from below, in the skating rink, with crowds and crowds of people listening, one heard, right through the night, those deep strong voices singing the familiar hymns.

Christmas had been, as she remembered it, a private and interior, a family, almost a dynastic affair, with the larger houses, the larger families, the aunts and the cousins, the uncles and the grandparents all gathered together so enormously well provided for and at ease in their secluded world, the Christmas happiness spreading from heart to heart and a sense prevailing that the Lord blessed every gift and every grandchild.

Heavens, the joy was truly terrifying, sitting here with eyes upturned, as though those candles, those brightly colored baubles, those green boughs and tiny scintillations, one behind another, and Christmas bell and ball and star, reflecting, flashing back the happiness, were saying, 'This is, my little one, the tree – the mystic tree of joy on earth. Behold it hung with candy cane and cornucopia, with dolls and skates and ponies, with little dogs and donkeys and darling pets to be your very own, hung, in fact, with all you ever asked your parents to bestow upon you. But do not snatch, my little one; for there upon the radiant tip of your miraculous tree, behold – the Christmas angel, the trumpets, and the wings outspread; see, all the candles lighted for the festival.'

She used to sit wide-eyed and gaze. She did not grab or even touch a single bauble; and what images went through her mind she would not now be able to recall – perhaps Santa Claus with all his packs and presents, his reindeer shaking Christmas bells – a sense of waiting on miraculous occurrences, being there and not being there, and thinking very likely of more mysterious things, of forests far away and snowflakes falling, and maybe squirrels, rabbits, snowbirds, antelopes.

And she would not now have recognized one festival occasion as differing from the others, all merging in her mind to brew this Christmas ravishment, had it not been that, searching through her memories, she remembered the little lifted and exalted sense she'd had of something beautiful past comprehension going on that night between Aunt Adelaide and the delightful, the almost too fascinating young man with his auburn heard and periwinkle-blue eyes, so soon to become her Uncle Philip, making this Christmas Eve stand out for her as more important, somehow, than any other she had known.

Dressed in her sheer white frock with its blue sash and in her white silk stockings and her patent-leather pumps, there'd been something about the way she'd felt – six sleek shining curls hanging over her shoulders, down her back – that had given her, starched and soaped and scented as she was, and standing there among the cousins and the uncles and the aunts (each and every one of whom confirmed her in it, with their smiles and acquiescent nods), a sense of waiting, angelically prepared, on ceremonials of a nature far surpassing earthly joy.

They were turning off the gas in the hall, in the dining room; someone behind her, and on tiptoe, was putting out first one lamp and then another. The light on the stairs had been extinguished. There was the encircling dark, the all-pervasive hush. And everyone (and all together) drawing in their breath. The double doors between the two large rooms were rolling back; and then, as though escaping from everyone at once, the great, the general 'Oooh' – the 'Aah, how *beautiful!*'

And was she taking the hand of her Aunt Adelaide, arrayed in cloudy gray and silver while Aunt Adelaide's companion, in all his elegance of shining shirtfront and surprising auburn beard, held her other hand and urged her to look at it, just to look at it – or was she standing there apart, alone, the rapturous 'aah' still warm upon her lips, struck dumb and speechless by the wonder?

There stood the tree – the great, the green, the fabulous hemlock – with all its layered boughs reaching out into the room, filling it with greenness, tapering upward, till its tip almost, but not quite, touched the ceiling, and distributing a Christmas incense which the warmth of the room, the heat of burning candles drew out to such a fine intensity of Christmas sentiment. There it stood before her, garlanded, looped round with ropers of snow-white popcorn, with rainbow-colored chains of paper bracelets, with silver tinsel and with gold, hung with blue and red and gold and with silver balls and bells and silver stars so cunningly faceted as to receive and flash back, from bell and ball, from star and candle flame, from the upper and the nether ornaments and trinkets so many tiny sparks and scintillations, so many beams and filaments of light, as to create in all the boughs and branches a mesh and maze of brightness, the candles with the blue candle-centers all together flickering, traveling upward to a point of highest ecstasy.

There it stood, fixing her in a trance, rendering her incapable of detaching this little picture from that, or one moment from the next – kneeling or sitting down, smiling, getting up, walking round, around, the blessed instants blending, melting one into another, becoming, and even as she gazed, memory, message, meaning.

For here, under the white sheet spread out to save the carpet from candle grease and hemlock needles, were all the

Christmas gifts, of every shape and size, wrapped with white or silver paper, tied with white or red or silver ribbons, embellished with holly and mistletoe and inscribed with loving dedications – 'Hilly from Mamma and Papa'; 'Hilly, Merry Christmas from Uncle Theodore'; 'John from Aunt Sally'; 'Hilly from Mamma and Papa'; 'Adelaide from her father' – and all and everybody searching to find their own particular presents – package heaped on package, and each one for somebody, with love from someone else, and all presumably from Santa Claus.

And oh, the smile and grace and glance and gesture of it – this charming episode and that, the voices, the salutations, while the walls of the two big rooms faded away into dim corners and that sense, with the snowflakes pit-patting on the windowpanes, of the snow accumulating outdoors, of the mystical preparation for tomorrow fringing her thoughts with such a strangeness, such a flame of joy. And not being at all certain whether she was unwrapping her own Christmas presents or assisting at the unwrapping of someone else's – being so lost in the idea that everybody was kissing, or receiving, or giving or thanking, hearing so many exclamations; Aunt Bessie crying out to Uncle Lucien, 'How *could* you have known?' and her mother embracing her father and taking a small slip of paper out of a tiny envelope, declaring that it was *far* too much; he should *never* have thought of such a thing; and old Mrs Constable trying to tell her something about a piebald pony, just arrived and waiting in the stable, and not at all sure that she hadn't seen it, saddled with silver and bridled with gold, drawing a little jeweled pony carriage round and round the room; but on the other hand not at all certain that she had. For was she not carrying a miraculous doll that opened and closed its lids and said distinctly, 'Mamma-Papa' whenever you pulled a string hidden beneath its long lace petticoats; and hadn't Aunt Adelaide's companion just plucked from the Christmas tree a little darling candy cane and a cornucopia filled with Christmas candy and presented her with both; and was she not at the moment sucking a barley Santa Claus, walking round and round and thinking happily how the world for many days to come would be a perfect paradise of spun sugar and chocolate bonbons and wondrously striped and twisted ribbon candy?

And, moreover, wasn't she all the time and at every moment wondering whether her beautiful, her beloved Aunt Adelaide was 'in love.' The words (she had heard them for the first time in her life on the lips of her Uncle Archie – 'head over heels in love with the fellow') running in and out of her mind together with all manner of hints and intimations as to what they really meant. And if a part of this hallowed Christmas was having her Aunt Adelaide in love with this delightful creature with his auburn beard and strange blue eyes, she was determined to lay herself open to every breath and beam and smile of their condition. And this need they both displayed of being in her society, and so tremendously happy as they were, was almost, she felt, as though they'd wished to use a little girl in a white dress and a blue sash, with bright hair and eyes, as a kind of medium – a way of saying to each other that perhaps some day they too might be possessed of just such a little treasure of their own.

And now they'd gone off and left her with her doll, her speculations and her barley sugar. And was this just another of these Christmas fantasies, hung up like magic-lantern pictures in her mind (her doll in its lace petticoats, the pony prancing round the room)? There, without a doubt, was her white-haired Great-aunt Sarah, in a velvet dress and with a paper cap upon her head, waltzing about the room with her handsome papa; and that was her grandfather, holding in front of him and with an expression of absolute astonishment a pair of pink pajamas. And had she, or had she not, caught that glimpse of them in the deep bay of the windows and behind the marble statue of Susanna – the gentleman bending over Aunt Adelaide, taking her in his arms, kissing her so fervently on the lips? All was shift and change and one bright tableau imposed upon another. But surely the little hoarded sense she had of the way these two had been behaving all the evening was part of the strange, the quite unearthly happiness now spreading in her heart.

For in the next room they had gathered round the piano – Mamma and Papa, Grandpa, the cousins, the aunts and uncles, old Mrs Constable – while the familiar words, all bright and touched with an angelic gravity, came floating in to her:

> *'O little town of Bethlehem!*
> *How still we see thee lie –'*

carried back through all the years and being there in person in those dark and silent streets, while overhead the stars silently, so silently, passed by; and receiving one by one those Bethlehem pictures – Mary and Joseph kneeling there in the stable, and Jesus in the manger with the crown of light around His little head. And then – the chords breaking, the tune changing –

> *'Silent night, holy night,*
> *All is calm, all is bright –'*

received again into the Here, the Now, and appreciating with such rapture that, outside these brightly lighted windows, and all in commemoration of that miracle accomplished centuries ago, the clouds had cleared, the night was blue and frosty underneath the Christmas sky –

> *'It came upon the midnight clear,*
> *That glorious song of old –'*

discovering a cow, a wise man, a shepherd, and there, somewhat higher up, the Infant Jesus; and finally lifting her eyes, beholding on the top of the fabulous tree and raising silver trumpets to his lips the herald angel with his wings outspread –

> *'Hark! the herald angels sing*
> *Glory to the new-born King –'*

And could there be imagined, wondered Mrs Danforth, stopping again in front of her little grandson, a joy so pure, so bright, so inaccessible?

christmas foods

You soon know what bird is roasting, for most of them make a brisk, spluttering sound in the oven, but goose makes rich, ruminative sounds like pouring oil out of a can, or a very fat man seeing a joke an hour later.

RACHEL FERGUSON

Sue Arnold
(contemporary)

Sue Arnold was born in India and is half Burmese. She was educated in England and at Trinity College Dublin. She started her career as a journalist at the *Lancaster Evening Telegraph* and has also worked for the *Teheran Journal*, the *Independent* and the *Evening Standard*. She is currently radio critic for the *Observer*. She has written two other books, both works of non-fiction: *Little Princes*, about royal children, and *A Burmese Legacy*. Sue Arnold has six children and lives in London.

This article on the Christmas turkey industry was published in *Curiouser and Curiouser: the Best of Sue Arnold* in 1985.

It is time to talk turkey again. It is time to ponder, as I do every year, whether the traditional Christmas bird is not a tedious and tiresome commodity, to be seasoned and stuffed and stitched and trussed and basted and tested and heaved in and out of the oven with breaking back and sweating brow and sinking heart; for in my long experience, no matter how you cosset and care for the brute, no matter how you robe it with voluptuous bacon brassières and serve it garnished like an over-dressed dowager with watercress and chipolatas, the result is always the same – a pale plank of reconstituted chipboard in the name of breast, or a wodge of oaken sinew hewn from one gargantuan thigh. Is it really worth it?

Only once in my life have I tasted a turkey that made me lick my lips and call for more. That was in Dublin at the home of a very dear friend. It was Boxing Day as I recall and, resigned to the inevitable spread of cold sawdust with Cumberland sauce, I was astounded at the succulent, tangy morsels of cold roast fowl that she heaped upon my plate. What was the secret?

Well, she said, it was a home grown bird, slaughtered ten days before Christmas by the local farmer, left to hang in his shed like a pheasant for a week and then stuffed with a couple of pounds of rough old beef shin or maybe shank. Thereafter it was cooked at a spanking pace in a turf-fired oven, the beef moistening and flavouring the meat in the process.

I should perhaps mention that it was the same friend who sent her cousin in England a turkey one Christmas. Delighted, the cousin loaded it straight into the oven on Christmas morning. Scarcely had the family returned from church, their appetites pleasantly whetted by the aromas exuding from the kitchen, when there was a great explosion within. The door of the oven had blown off, the turkey lay in tatters and buried deep within the nether cavity were the splintered remains of a bottle of poteen, secreted there to foil Her Majesty's Customs and Excise.

But tradition dies hard at Schloss Arnold, and I was gloomily resigning myself to the annual turkey drag when someone told me of an extraordinary phenomenon known as the self-basting turkey. Be warned, said my source, there are many self-basting birds on the market but only one, the Golden Norfolk, bastes with real dairy butter. A curious picture loomed before me of a semi-comatose bird soaking in my roasting tin like a weary wing-forward in the bath after a match, occasionally lifting an arm to dowse its limbs with the surrounding liquor.

Fool, said my source, they inject under its skin.

Good grief, I said, isn't that painful?

All of which preamble explains my presence recently at Great Witchingham in Norfolk, headquarters of Mr Bernard Matthews, the undisputed Napoleon of the turkey business. Mr Matthews produces more than five million turkeys every year for the table, half of which he sells as deep-frozen whole roasting birds, with or without the butter infusion. The rest he processes into deep-frozen turkey burgers, turkey sausages and a handy little number called the turkey roll. Mr Matthews started thirty years ago as an insurance clerk with twenty turkey eggs which he bought at an auction for £1. His business now has an annual turnover of £40 million – truly a tale of enterprise and dedication to warm the cockles of the deepest frozen hearts.

Alas for time and space to tell you the half of what I witnessed in Great Witchingham – the 30,000 eggs set every day in giant incubators, the day-old chicks travelling along conveyor belts like airline passengers on moving walkways, the deep litter houses full of turkey stags crying 'gobble gobble' in unison at visitors. And then the plant itself where every year 100,000 tons of turkey meat are processed by butchers wearing red and yellow crash-helmets, flinging spare parts into huge drums to be turned miraculously into twenty-foot lengths of deep frozen turkey roll like pink telegraph poles.

Afterwards Mr Matthews offered frankfurters made of turkey, streaky bacon made of turkey, smoked ham made of turkey and, the *pièce de resistance* for me, a whole cold roast turkey made entirely of boneless white meat which could be sliced like a loaf of bread. If my host had offered plum pudding and brandy butter made entirely from turkey feathers, I would not have been surprised.

I have just cooked my first Golden Norfolk self-basting turkey. Even as I write this I can hear it sizzling agreeably behind closed doors. It looks good, it smells good, and if the couple of pounds of rough old beef soaked in poteen that I carefully stuffed it with have worked their promised magic, I have no doubt that it will taste not unticklesome to the palate withal.

Spasenija Markovich
(*fl.* early 20th century)

Little is known about the Serbian writer Spasenija Markovich but, judging by the text of her 800-page work, *My Cookbook* (1939), she must have been very dedicated and extremely knowledgeable. Mira Crouch, who translated sections of the book reprinted here, explained that it was given to her mother by her father, but it did not get much use because the world was on the verge of war and consequent food shortages. Crouch adds, 'My mother lugged the book halfway across the world to Australia for sentimental reasons, and I hang on to it, too, for old times' sake. I have occasionally used a recipe or two, but on the whole, they are too demanding (in more ways than one – many of the recipes for cakes start with "take 18 eggs . . .").'

Markovich's preface to the book, written in February 1939, notes that the 'terrible war' (World War I) had changed women's lives, showing that they were capable of more than their traditional duties, which they now approached in a different spirit.

History, however, can throw some light on the symbolic meaning of the traditional Serbian Christmas as described in Markovich's book. The southern Slavs were converted to Christianity during AD 500–700; before that time, their culture was based on beliefs in sylvan deities and spirits of the then heavily forested Balkans, and the Christian rituals still incorporate elements of that old culture. Hospitality extended to passing travellers is an important custom, possibly stemming from the cultural memory of a people who were on the move for centuries from the Carpathian mountains (the original homeland of all Slavs) to the Balkans. Thus the Christmas morning visitor, as described below, may be taken to be the symbolic traveller, at once stranger and family member. He is also a young man and thus, metaphorically, a sign of strength, prosperity and freedom, since young men had, for centuries, been a scarce resource because of the constant uprisings against the occupying Turks. In 500 years of Turkish rule, men with guns would mostly have been in hiding, coming out into the open only to fight for freedom. Gunshots in the village square, then, would have signalled the freeing of the village from Turkish occupation.

The following edited extract from *My Cookbook* describes the traditional Serbian Christmas, where Christmas Eve falls on January 6th, according to the Diocletian calendar still observed by the Eastern Christian Church. In general, the description refers to the traditional village setting; from the late nineteenth century onwards, city households increasingly adopted a much reduced version of the various rituals involved.

Traditional Christmas begins on Christmas Eve when the floor of the whole house is covered in straw. Early in the morning, the housewife covers the table in the 'main' room (i.e. the dining room) with a white linen cloth in the middle of which she places the Christmas candle (tall, thick wax candle) and a copper dish with four red apples in it, on top of which she puts the freshly baked Christmas yeast bun. The householder then sprinkles wheat over the bun, as well as corn, silver coins and prunes and walnuts – all symbols of plentitude from the land and a good life in the home.

During the day, the housewife prepares a festive evening meal traditionally eaten cold; fried fish, dried bean salad, brown rice, pickled cabbage in olive oil, various other pickles (onions, capsicums, green tomatoes), and, for sweets, noodles with grated walnuts and sugar, honey and stewed prunes and apples. (Note: this is a fasting meal – no milk, eggs or animal, though fish is allowed.) At the start of the meal, the head of the household (father, or grandfather if the latter is around) makes the sign of the cross over the table while holding walnuts, which are then placed one in each corner of the room, where they remain for the duration of the holiday (three days). (The walnuts represent the Christian world, as they signify east, west, north and south.) Only after that do other members of the household sit down at the table, at which point the head of the house lights the candle and the Christmas hymn ('Christ is Born') is sung.

The Christmas fire already burns in the hearth. Early that day, the householder would have gone into the forest and cut down a tree (birch, usually) and prepared it for the evening fire by spreading honey over the cut wood. The householder lights the fire before dinner as the family assembles; he ritually embraces and kisses each member of the household as the sparks begin to fly. The fire is kept alive all night, tended by the householder who also looks after the Christmas spit (a pig especially fattened for the holiday) which takes the whole night of basting and turning to cook. The meat is ready early on Christmas morning, when the householder slices off and tastes the first morsel to break the fast and thus to signify the start of the festivities. These begin with a special visit from a young male relative – a symbol of strength and protection for the family. (Often there used to be competition among young men for visits to particularly esteemed families, sometimes the sub-text being the courting of a daughter of the house.) He announces his visit by firing a few shots from his hunting gun, just outside the house. He then greets the householder, saying: 'Christ is born!' And the householders replies 'verily He is born!' The two men then visit the spit and have a taste of the meat, after which they enter the house, where the visitor stokes the fire, tosses wheat and silver coins all over the room and chants well-wisher incantations about health, happiness and prosperity for the whole family. The visitor remains with the household for the day, which starts with the lady of the house giving him a piece of the Christmas bun and the householder gifting him with money. After that the whole family goes to church, where, as well as the service, much greeting and chatting take place.

Later, people drop in for visits and there is always an extended family gathering for the festive meal at lunchtime.

There is a special loaf which is placed beside the candle (still burning on the table from the night before), and at the start of the meal this is broken up by the housewife; she gives a piece each to those present (and it is considered particularly fortunate if there is a travelling stranger who has unexpectedly turned up and has been invited to share the meal; needless to say, many destitute persons have benefitted from this custom. The bread contains a silver coin, and whoever happens to get the coin keeps it and looks after it, as it is his/her lucky charm for a whole year. If a member of the household (rather than a guest) gets the coin, it is given to the householder for safe keeping; he places it in the corner of the frame around the household's patron saint icon.

The Christmas meal starts with chicken soup (actually a sort of thick stew with lots of vegetables, meat etc and served with sour cream or yoghurt), then 'sarma' (pickled cabbage rolls stuffed with meat and rice), then the barbecued pig with sundry salads and crusty bread, and then a walnut pie (using filo pastry – much like baklava) and, of course, wine, and sweet strong coffee in little pots at the end of the meal.

Catherine Maria Fanshawe
(1765–1834)

Catherine Maria Fanshawe was a physically frail but intellectually robust member of a small set of London intellectuals. She painted and etched with as much facility as she wrote. Her poems were printed for private circulation in 1865, but the only piece widely remembered is a riddle on the letter 'H' which has often been attributed falsely to Lord Byron:

> 'Twas whispered in heaven,
> 'twas muttered in hell.

The poem that appears here is heavily ironic, and appears to praise festive domesticity above intellectual and artistic pursuits.

Answer to a Letter from the Hon. Mrs. Pole Carew, in which she had said 'I am very happy, and care every day less for poetry and painting, and more for cookery and poultry.'

> Blest be the day that on your book of life
> Stamp't the fair title of a happy wife!
> Blest be the hand that, arm'd with virtuous rage,
> Tore thence, or cancell'd, every useless page,
> Renounc'd the pomps of vanities and wit,
> Poultry inscribed where Poetry was writ,
> Painting (unprofitable art) effaced,
> And gave to Cookery all your thoughts on taste;
> Who deck those altars, feed no transient flame,
> Nor solid pudding change for empty fame.
> May each revolving year your joys increase,
> With added flocks of guinea fowls and geese;
> On countless eggs may ducks and pigeons sit!
> And all attain the honours of the spit!
> Chickens in multitudes be hatch'd, and oh!
> May no chill autumn lay your turkies low;
> Their tender lives, ye felon foxes, spare!
> Make them, ye poultry maids, your hourly care!
> So their plump forms your Christmas feasts shall
>   crown,
> Well trussed and roasted of a lively brown;
> Boiling is spoiling; but, if boil they must,
> To insipidity itself be just.
> O'er their pale limbs be creamy currents pour'd,
> And the rich sauce stand plenteous on your board;

See round your shores th' instructive lesson float,
Within the oyster, and without the boat;
Ocean your measure, but avoid its fault;
Make not your sauce so thin, nor half so salt.

Happy, whom thus domestic pleasures fix,
Blest with one husband, and with many chicks

Isabella Beeton
(1836–65)

Familiarly known as plain Mrs Beeton, Isabella Beeton was educated at Heidelberg in Germany and became an accomplished pianist, but she is remembered principally as a cookery writer. In 1856 she married the publisher Samuel Orchard Beeton and contributed articles to his journal *The Englishwoman's Domestic Magazine*. She spent four years completing her celebrated manual, *Book of Household Management*, over a thousand pages long and containing not only recipes but numerous tips and advice on all areas of domestic science. It was published in 1861. Mrs Beeton died after the birth of her fourth son. Her recipe for 'very good' Christmas plum pudding appears below.

INGREDIENTS 1½ lb of raisins, ½ lb of currants, ¾ lb of bread-crumbs, ½ lb of mixed peel, ¾ lb of suet, 8 eggs, 1 wineglassful of brandy.

MODE Stone and cut the raisins in halves, but do not chop them; wash, pick and dry the currants, and mince the suet finely; cut the candied peel into thin slices, and grate down the bread into fine crumbs.

When all these dry ingredients are prepared, mix them well together; then moisten the mixture with the eggs, which should be well beaten, and the brandy; stir well, that everything may be very thoroughly blended, and *press* the pudding into a buttered mould; tie it down tightly with a floured cloth, and boil for five or six hours. It may be boiled in a cloth without a mould, and will require the same time allowed for cooking.

As Christmas puddings are usually made a few days before they are required for table, when the pudding is taken out of the pot, hang it up immediately, and put a plate or saucer underneath to catch the water that may drain from it. The day it is to be eaten, plunge it into boiling water, and keep it boiling for at least two hours; then turn it out of the mould, and serve with brandy sauce. On Christmas Day a sprig of holly is usually placed in the middle of the pudding and about a wine-glassful of brandy poured round it, which at the moment of serving, is lighted and the pudding thus brought to the table encircled in flame.

Average cost 4s. *Sufficient* for a quart mould for seven or eight persons. Seasonable on the 25th December, and on various festive occasions till March.

Rachel Ferguson
(1893–1957)

Rachel Ferguson was born in Hampton Wick but moved to Kensington when she was a child and lived there until she died. Despite a privileged background, as a young woman she became a radical and active campaigner for women's suffrage, numbering Emmeline, Sylvia and Christabel Pankhurst among her circle. She worked for the Women's Social and Political Union (having established a teenage branch of it, The Young Purple White and Green Club), acting in fundraising plays and sketches. She trained at the Academy of Dramatic Art, but her career on the stage was cut short by World War I, after which she devoted herself to writing full time. She had always been interested in literature; her first novel, she explained in her 1958 autobiography *We Were Amused*, was written at the age of ten, and called *Hellass of the Gates of Flame*. Ferguson worked as a drama critic and a columnist (Rachel for *Punch*) while writing novels, which were often centred on Edwardian middle-class family life depicted as a comedy of ridiculous manners. Her second book, *The Brontës Went to Woolworths* (1931), was the one that established her popularity. Her other titles include *False Goddesses* (1923), *Sara Skelton* (1929) and *Popularity's Wife* (1932). She devoted her later years to animal welfare and support for decayed gentlewomen.

This extract from *Memoirs of a Fir Tree, The Life of Elsa Tannenbaum* (1946) recounts the gourmandising of a German Christmastide from a tree's point of view. Christmas was clearly of great sentimental interest to Ferguson. In her autobiography she recalls a childhood Christmas in a neighbour's nursery when the lady of the house made an enormous snowball with a domed lid, into which a small child was packed. The guests stood in a circle and called for Father Christmas to appear. He did, with gifts for everyone.

German children don't hang up their stockings, although Christmas Eve is made more of over here than Christmas Day itself. And families don't have their presents on the breakfast table, but each person has a separate table in the Salon on which their things are heaped. So there is none of that embarrassment I've noticed in England when presents are opened in turn and before the whole family, because if you have your own table you can have a good rummage and a nice private time of it all, and keep the worst things to the last and examine them without your expression slipping publicly. (Some people seem fated to give the worst presents, always, and it's nothing to do with what money they have, either.)

Then everyone goes to church, where the Pastor dresses very plainly in black, and never puts on those pretty embroidered bell-pulls the English clergymen do. When I first came to England, I thought a surplice was a night-shirt and that the Herr Pastor had got up terribly late for church and rung the bell so vigorously for his shaving-water that it fell down round his neck and he had to come as he was. But I know better, now.

And the service is much longer than in England and not nearly so lively, but full of *Chorále*, which aren't the same as Carols, and the people stand or sit for prayers and don't keeping going on their knees.

And perhaps because the service is so long, the midday meal which follows it is almost longer, and you have to have your health and strength to weather it, I assure you.

It nearly always starts with plates of soup, and lots of it, and being so English myself I've quite lost my taste for it. For into it go the most complicated and improbable things, like cabbage with beetroot and cream. Then there is usually a huge, long brown loin of pork served with well-vinegared red cabbage, or veal cutlet, both of which the Germans adore, as well as the festival dish which isn't turkey, but goose stuffed with chestnuts and herbs and served with cranberry sauce, and perhaps another cabbage stuffed with minced meat or carroway seeds. You soon know what bird is roasting, for most of them make a brisk, spluttering sound in the oven, but goose makes rich, ruminative sounds like pouring oil out of a can, or a very fat man seeing a joke an hour later.

Glupple . . . glupple . . . glupple

Even naturalised German ladies can't help sounding rather like it, themselves, when they discuss the menu in English in the days before the feast, for they say 'Rrrrrrroast goose,' just like that.

On the sideboard of the richer families there is also a fine smoked ham with fat that *crumbles* (I still don't quite feel that Crumbling is properly understood, in England). Sometimes it is cured in wine, sometimes, as in Westphalia, in black treacle. And flanking it, a smoked ox-tongue, and perhaps a tall stoneware jar of truffled liver.

Then the puddings! There is the Tree-cake (a *Baumkuchen*), which is a log-shaped iced sponge, and there is, perhaps, an *Apfeltorte* – a great, open apple flan with sultanas and citron peel, and to wind up with, to say nothing of the good wines, cups of coffee heaped with whipped cream.

And then come *us*. And lest the family considers itself under-nourished still, there is something to eat for all, hung on our boughs: slabs of honeycake that looks so deceptively like gingerbread; the pink or white luck-bringing sugar pigs, with *Ich Bringe Glück* in gilt letters on their fat sides, and boxes, round or heart-shaped, of solid marzipan, pale pink, green or yellow, iced in the centre and decorated with a greeting. And there are ornaments, too, of sugary biscuit with frills of macaroon-paper and a picture scrap in the middle, besides gilded walnuts, and little sugar birdcages with net walls and a dab of yellow sugar inside for the canary. And I mustn't forget the shiny cardboard horns lined with coloured tissue paper and tied with silk ribbons, full of chocolates – a horn for everybody, which are snipped off and handed out when the principal gifts have been distributed.

On the top of us, where our hat would be if we were out-doors, was fixed, not a fairy doll, but the Christchild, a wax baby doll with real flaxen hair and a gilt halo.

The older people sometimes have Christmas music, and they sing *Heilige Nacht, Stille Nacht*, to a lullaby tune, in memory of the Holy Night. And that is a comfortable, drowsy melody, too. Or there are trios and quartettes of flute, viola, piano and violin or 'cello, and the children sometimes curtsey to us, and are stolid little angels of good behaviour – until the marzipan gets in its work, and they are removed, roaring, to bed.

And then a large tray is brought in, heaped with hot rolls stuffed with ham or liver sausage or smoked salmon, and more cake, and jugs of hot grog and iced beer. And whitewood boxes of our famous Elvas plums, small and deep purple and deliciously acid-sweet, are handed round.

And the toys! It isn't often that I've had cause to pity English children, for they seem to get everything they want, these days, if they whine long and loud enough. And I have heard even their mothers say that all this Priority business is making them grow up selfish, greedy, and with far too big an idea of their own importance. But I can feel sorry for all that they have missed in the way of playthings. And it is an awful thought that children born in 1937 have literally never seen what I call a toy, for first of all they were too small to appreciate what they had, and then the war came, bringing with it dolls I wouldn't tolerate on my branches, for they are not only dressed in what looks like old kettleholders, but are unnecessarily ugly into the bargain, and deformed as well. And there seems to be nothing else, except bricks and puzzles, and models of everything to remind the nurseries that there was a big and terrible war going on in which they were made to join by presents of tanks, gas-masks and tommy-guns.

My needles drop even to think of it. You see, I am used to pretty dolls with real hair and eyelashes, and eyes which close, and dainty dresses. And to musical-boxes no bigger than a large-sized pill-box, with a picture on the lid, which tinkle out tunes when the handle is turned; and sledges made of cotton-wool, and silvered, with a little man inside; and to a model village with shops and churches and houses, and villagers passing across the street to another tune when you turn the handle, and to the red-and-blue tin ball on a string which, when whirled, sends out coloured sparks; and to the little feathered hen who pecks up grain when set in motion, and to the green velvet cauliflower that, when wound, plays a tune and sends up a white rabbit from inside . . .

Things like that . . .

Well, well . . . We hope so much it will all be again as once it was. Life isn't all Hitler. And I will tell you this: *The Best Families in Germany did not recognise him.* He was not *hochwohlgeboren*, but what the French call *canaille* and you call a bounder. He was not received among us all before the war. We have a tremendous feeling for these things; you may call it snobbery if you like, but I think it is proper pride of birth and a sense of values. And as for Herr Hitler, even we Tannenbaums would not have cared to invite him to pine-kernels and mushrooms. It would only have got *us* into the wrong set.

Yes, we hope for the old times back again, as you do. And what the German family really wants isn't war or even power, but roast goose and plenty of it, glittering things to look at – and us, the Tannenbaums. And I think now you have won the war you will, in time, let us have them once more.

Janie Mitchell
(1968–)

Janie Mitchell was born in Birmingham and raised in Shropshire. She left England in 1990 after university and lived in Paris, where she taught English and busked, and in Oregon, where she was a recording artist with New Weave Records. In 1993, she went to Romania to meet the Revolution's poets and had her poetry broadcast by Lilliana Ursu on national radio. She returned to London, where she now lives, to complete a Masters degree in Critical Theory at Goldsmiths College. Her poems have been published in the *Swansea Review*, *Poetry Wales*, and the anthologies *The Path From The Year's Height* (Border Poets) and *Needs Be* (Flarestack Press). She has appeared at the Hay and Ledbury festivals and has written a travel book about swimming. This poem is called 'Spoiling the Broth'.

My Dalston-Market bantam bobs, almost revived,
between the jars of Dad's pickled cabbage and Mom's
cranberry sauce, nesting itself in wrapping paper.

Mothers flitter like tinsel under the streetlights,
winding up last minute trimmings. I'm a walking
hamper, bottom of the wardrobe, under the stairs –

the nooks the Big Day hides the day before. Liverpool
Street, I heave two courses onto the Tube, worried
my dead bird's growing warm and the pudding

Mom stirred and steamed in Summer is splitting its
    foil.
Queensway, Christmas will not come. Arabs and
    tourists,
open casinos, Thai restaurants clammy with atheists

and orphans. Katia's flat above the throngs in Pizza
    Hut
is tree and fairy lightless. She tells me how much
    she's spent.
We drink the sherry my parents left me (before they
    flew

to Italy) to heat the hallways. (My family home
is empty for the first time. There would be snow there.
A candlelit service. The only night the church is
    warm.)

There's a Bosnian girl I've bought organic bath salts.
We've never met. In the morning, too late for the
    Serpentine
swim, I say 'One does not give to receive' as she takes
    out

her purse. A Turk and a Chinese man arrive
with champagne (the 7–11's open then). Too many
    cooks,
we convene around the chicken. My bird, if not dead
    now

is stabbed to a spicy mess of a death: cloves and rind,
cinnamon sticks, rosemary sprigs. Molested wings,
    skin
paprika bruised. A final, insulting lemon is shoved

where Mom, for thirty-three years, has put a potato
(a quintessence of juices). Sausage stuffing vetoed,
I'll make the best of the gravy. But someone's chucked

the vegetable water. I say 'A Christmas dinner
without gravy is not a Christmas dinner' and storm out
to Hyde Park to watch the squabbling ducks. On a
    bench,

I say out loud 'Merry Christmas'. An American
couple stare like I am alone. I walk back to show
I am not. We eat in five minutes. Foreign tangs,

Sweet for sour, pips with bones. My confused tongue.
We save no meat for later sandwiches and Dad's
    pickles
go untasted. I'm somewhere else when the pudding

is scraped from its foil – like mud from a pail. No-one
    gets
to see it aflame, a perfect dome, a holy mountain of
    sultanas
and suet, brought in with the lights low and carols on.

It's spattered like muck in bowls of sorbet (Fatally, I
    left
it to someone else to buy cream, make brandy
    butter).
Nothing will do it justice now. The booze all drunk

(at home we'd have bottles to last till Easter), we play
the dictionary game. Someone reads a definition,
    others guess
the word. Everyone is quite good but I win. It's my
    mother

tongue, after all. Next year, I want to be at home. I
    root
through the bin for the wishbone, thrown away with
    a carcass
Mom would have boiled for Boxing Day soup.

Laurie Graham
(1947–)

Laurie Graham was born in Leicester. She studied sciences, married, and had four children. Her first novel, *The Man for the Job*, was published in 1987. For the next nine years she earned her living writing a series of best-selling survival guides, and as a regular contributor to national magazines and newspapers, before returning to writing fiction. *The Ten O'Clock Horses* was published in 1996, followed by *Perfect Meringues* and *The Future Homemakers of America*. In addition to novels, Graham also writes drama scripts for radio. She now lives in Venice.

'Papoo Yaya', previously unpublished, is a charming and poignant account of a family's Christmas preparations on a Greek island.

On our island, the saying went, there were three things a fisherman feared; the sea, fire, and women. Still, when the weather was too stormy for them to dance with the one old devil, somehow they found the courage to huddle at home with the other two. Not my Dad – he'd left the fishing and was getting good money, goat subsidies from Brussels – but my Papoo, and his friends, Thin George and Dimitri, because they had never known anything else. When the seas roared and flung their spray against the harbour wall, Papoo stayed home. He allowed Yaya to bring him coffee and throw wood on the fire, and Yaya allowed him to think there was nothing in the world she'd rather do, except on the days she was baking. On those days he was told to skedaddle because, as any woman would tell you, you can't make good bread with men under your feet.

So, any morning Papoo saw Yaya clearing the big tasselled cloth off the table and reaching down the flour, he knew he had to go to the café, play backgammon, steer clear of women and all that funny business with yeast.

Papoo and Yaya lived in the end of our house. First it was their house. Then, when Mama grew up and married my Dad, it became her house. 'And some day it'll be yours,' Mama used to say, because I was the oldest, and I was a girl. That's how things were on Arki. When the wedding music stopped, everyone moved along a room.

I was named Katerina, after my yaya, just as my mother was named Sophia, after hers. Sophia, Katerina, Sophia, Katerina, strung like beads along a branch of our family tree.

Yaya was as nimble as a kid and as strong as an ox. She could beat the rugs harder than anyone else and whitewash the walls faster. In the autumn, when she pruned the mulberry tree, she dared climb higher than any man, and when everything else was done, she'd fetch out her needlework and embroider tiny patterns with her coloured silks. No one could sew like Yaya. Especially me. Heavy hands, they said I had. Hot, grubby fingers that marked the cloth and knotted the thread and dropped the needle. 'Never be rid of that one' Papoo used to say. 'No one wants a wife who can't sew.' 'All the better for you,' I used to think, 'because when I marry, I shall need all this space for my big handsome husband and my big handsome telly, and the rest of you'll have to squeeze up a bit more. In the wood shed probably.' 'May you see your children's children' they sing at weddings.

But not too soon.

One day Yaya wasn't as strong as an ox anymore. Papoo reasoned with her that there was star-gazey fish needed pickling, and Dimitri's wife brought her special soup, and Tigri, who was merely a cat, but thought he was a tiger, weaved around the legs of the bed, but nothing helped. She closed her eyes and wouldn't open them again, not even when the priest came with his stove pipe hat and his holy oil.

So we wrapped her in a soft blanket and loaded her onto a cart. The priest walked before her, singing, and Thin George's donkey pulled her all the way up to the graveyard without once bucking or hollering or stopping for a bite to eat. We laid Yaya to rest, next to a Sophia, who lay next to another Katerina, and down below, the sea was the colour of violets. Dimitri's wife said the dead never had a better view, and Papoo said a virtuous woman's price was far above rubies, which was just about the nicest thing I ever heard him say. Then we all clambered back down the rough track, and that donkey pulled every donkey-stunt in the book.

Papoo stayed in his room at the end of our house. He ate his meals with us, but as soon as he'd wiped his plate he was on his feet and gone. Sometimes he took his boat out, but his heart didn't really seem in it. On the third day and the ninth day and the fortieth day the priest said prayers for Yaya. We all lit candles and fed the neighbours on boiled wheat with honey and pomegranate seeds, to speed her on her way. And afterwards Papoo always went for a long, stomping walk and I followed behind, just in case he needed anyone to talk to. Or any help. His moustache was so wide, sometimes I thought he might take off in the wind. Papoo, last seen cresting Stavrovouni and gaining altitude. Arki's first man in space. The week before Christmas he walked all the way to Horta and bought semolina flour and sugar, currants and cinnamon, sultanas and sesame seeds. Mama said he was a silly old fool because he knew she'd make enough Christmas bread for all of us, but he laid out his shopping on Yaya's table anyway and Dimitri and Thin George came round and looked at it.

He fetched out the tin plate with a blue rim and the chipped water glass, but after that he was stuck. That was where I came in handy. I knew exactly which saucers Yaya used to measure the sultanas and currants and which basin was just the right size for the sugar. I put them on the table for him and he grunted, which was his way of saying 'Thank you for your trouble.'

Two days passed, and Mama had started our Christmas bread, but all Papoo had was a table filled with plates and packages. He said he just wasn't ready to start. Every time he was asked, he said it, and every time Mama winked at me.

Then I was sent with yeast. A cube of it, in a cup. I told him it was the secret of bread. 'Any fool knows that,' he said. And all the time he was looking at it out of the corner of his eye. Tomorrow, he might bake, he said, if it wasn't good weather for fishing.

The women were busy cleaning their houses and making honey cakes, and pine nut stuffing for the turkey. When I went to call him for his lunch, Papoo was on one chair and the cup of yeast was on another, directly in front of him, each waiting for the other to make the first move. In Yaya's kitchen the chairs were all green. Except for the one that was pink.

I whispered to him, what to do next, but I forgot to mention draughts. That afternoon Papoo mixed a little of the yeast with water and flour, but he left it uncovered, where the wind whistles through the crack in the door, and the magic didn't work. The yeast was hibernating. When I went to fetch him for his dinner, he was talking to the ikon of St Nicholas. There wasn't a fisherman on Arki hadn't been saved from drowning by St Nicholas, but he didn't seem much help when it came to baking.

'Try again' I told him. 'Only keep it snug and warm because it's a living thing.' It's a hard thing to believe, I know, and Papoo definitely didn't. He gave me a long hard look and went with Thin George to play backgammon.

It was still dark when we heard Papoo screaming. We threw on our coats and ran to see whether it was the house that was on fire or the roof that had blown off. But all we found was

Papoo, in nothing but his nightshirt, gibbering and wailing and dancing around in the cold winter morning.

'The Thing' he said, 'has climbed out of its bowl.'

Mama said Dad should go inside and look, and Dad said we should send the cat in first. But Tigri suddenly remembered some urgent tiger business and ran away, so while they were arguing about it and trying hard not to laugh, I slipped into Papoo's room to see what I could see.

He was right. It had climbed out of the bowl. Up and over the side, and now it was creeping across the table towards his bed. Papoo had mixed enough flour and yeast to feed the five thousand. I gathered it up into the bowl and it made a sighing noise. I loved the smell of the yeasty beast.

'Everything under control' I told them, and after we'd saved Papoo from certain pneumonia with a big dash of coffee, a shot of brandy and two slices of cake with apricot jam, and the sun had dragged itself up over Stavrovouni, I went back with him to his room, to help him with his Christmas bread.

First you have to punch the dough. It resists you for a while. Then it softens, as though it's decided it likes your touch after all, and it grows smooth and shiny as silk. You mix in the fruits and the spices, and the juice from the oranges and the rind from the lemons. Then the fun begins. You flour your hands and flour the table and you give that dough the squeezing and pummelling of its life.

Papoo watched me. 'See?' I said. 'The harder you knead it, the better it'll taste.' He rolled up his sleeves and he took a turn, but he was too gentle. Still thought that yeast might jump up and bite him, probably. So I told him Yaya's trick.

How she'd pretend the dough was someone who'd really annoyed her. How she'd name it and slap it around and give it a good telling off. I didn't tell him whose name she sometimes called it.

It seemed to give him the right idea. First the dough was some dirty dog called Yannis who'd cheated him at cards in 1965. Then it was some shyster called Kourtakis who'd given him bad advice about goat subsidies. Papoo's face grew pink and sweat broke out on his forehead and his hair stood on end. The dough was kneaded enough, but he wasn't through yet. He still had a thing or two to say to Yaya, who'd been as loyal as a sheepdog and sharp as a tin tack, who'd been a pretty as a picture and noble as a queen, and then upped and left him with no one to warm his feet on or trim his moustache. Papoo cried and kneaded, and I just cried and we kneaded our tears into the bread.

Of course, there were some things about Yaya he didn't know. He'd never seen her rolling her pastry with her broom handle, lifting it and flipping it over and rolling it some more, until it was so thin you could see daylight through it. He'd never seen her do the dance of the seven dish cloths.

Mama had been stoking the fire with dry twigs. When we carried Papoo's loaves outside, the walls of the oven were glowing.

'Sesame seeds?' Mama asked, because it wasn't the usual thing. But everyone agreed, it was the best Christmas bread in living memory. Papoo Yaya, we called him after that. Papoo Yaya, the master-baker. 'Heavy hands' he said, next time he saw me puckering my stitches and leaving thumb marks on my sewing. 'We shall never be rid of that one.'

'Good news for you, then,' I said, 'Or are you in a hurry to sleep in the wood shed?'

'Bah!' he said. And he went off for a long stomping walk up the hill, to talk to Yaya and challenge the wind with his moustache.

mischief and malfeasance at christmas

Every year on Christmas day I like to tell my mother that I'm a lesbian, even though I'm not. It just gets everything going.

JENNY ECLAIR

Agatha Christie
(1890–1976)

Queen of the quintessentially English, 'country cottage' murder mystery, Agatha Christie was educated by her mother, who encouraged her to read widely. Under the name of her first husband, Colonel Christie, whom she divorced in 1928, Agatha Christie wrote more than 70 classic detective novels, featuring the Belgian detective Hercule Poirot, or the village spinster, Miss Marple. Many of her stories were turned into West End productions and feature films. *The Mousetrap* in particular is famous for its record-breaking run. She also wrote under the pen-name of Mary Westmacott. Her own mysterious disappearance in the 1920s received much publicity. She was eventually found in Yorkshire, a victim of amnesia, or perhaps the author of her own mischievous plot. Christie married the archaeologist Sir Max Mallowan in 1930 and accompanied him on some of his expeditions, weaving some of the exotic locations into stories such as *Murder in Mesopotamia* (1936) and *Death on the Nile* (1937).

This extract from *Hercule Poirot's Christmas* (1938) suggests why the festive season may just be the most dangerous time of the year.

'Nothing like a wood fire,' said Colonel Johnson as he threw on an additional log and then drew his chair nearer to the blaze. 'Help yourself,' he added, hospitably calling attention to the tantalus and siphon that stood near his guest's elbow.

The guest raised a polite hand in negation. Cautiously he edged his own chair nearer to the blazing logs, though he was of the opinion that the opportunity for roasting the soles of one's feet (like some mediæval torture) did not offset the cold draught that swirled round the back of the shoulders.

Colonel Johnson, Chief Constable of Middleshire, might be of the opinion that nothing could beat a wood fire, but Hercule Poirot was of opinion that central heating could and did every time!

'Amazing business, that Cartwright case,' remarked the host reminiscently. 'Amazing man! Enormous charm of manner. Why, when he came here with you, he had us all eating out of his hand.'

He shook his head.

'We'll never have anything like that case!' he said. 'Nicotine poisoning is rare, fortunately.'

'There was a time when you would have considered all poisoning unEnglish,' suggested Hercule Poirot. 'A device of foreigners! Unsportsmanlike!'

'I hardly think we could say that,' said the chief constable. 'Plenty of poisoning by arsenic – probably a good deal more than has ever been suspected.'

'Possibly, yes.'

'Always an awkward business, a poisoning case,' said Johnson. 'Conflicting testimony of the experts – then doctors are usually so extremely cautious in what they say. Always a difficult case to take to jury. No, if one *must* have murder (which heaven forbid!) give me a straightforward case. Something where there's no ambiguity about the cause of death.'

Poirot nodded.

'The bullet wound, the cut throat, the crushed-in skull? It is there your preference lies?'

'Oh, don't call it a preference, my dear fellow. Don't harbour the idea that I *like* murder cases! Hope I never have another. Anyway, we ought to be safe enough during your visit.'

Poirot began modestly:

'My reputation –'

But Johnson had gone on.

'Christmas time,' he said. 'Peace, goodwill – and all that kind of thing. Goodwill all around.'

Hercule Poirot leaned back in his chair. He joined his fingertips. He studied his host thoughtfully.

He murmured: 'It is, then, your opinion that Christmas time is an unlikely season for crime?'

'That's what I said.'

'Why?'

'Why?' Johnson was thrown slightly out of his stride. 'Well, as I've just said – season of good cheer, and all that!'

Hercule Poirot murmured:

'The British, they are so sentimental!'

Johnson said stoutly: 'What if we are? What if we do like the old ways, the old traditional festivities? What's the harm?'

'There is no harm. It is all most charming! But let us for a moment examine *facts*. You have said that Christmas is a season of good cheer. That means, does it not, a lot of eating and drinking? It means, in fact, the *over*eating! And with the overeating there comes the indigestion! And with the indigestion there comes the irritability!'

'Crimes,' said Colonel Johnson, 'are not committed from irritability.'

'I am not so sure! Take another point. There is, at Christmas, a spirit of goodwill. It is, as you say, "the thing to do." Old quarrels are patched up, those who have disagreed consent to agree once more, even if it is only temporarily.'

Johnson nodded.

'Bury the hatchet, that's right.'

Poirot pursued his theme:

'And families now, families who have been separated throughout the year, assemble once more together. Now under these conditions, my friend, you must admit that there will occur a great amount of *strain*. People who do not *feel* amiable are putting great pressure on themselves to *appear* amiable! There is at Christmas time a great deal of *hypocrisy*, honourable hypocrisy, hypocrisy undertaken *pour le bon motif, c'est entendu*, but nevertheless hypocrisy!'

'Well, I shouldn't put it quite like that myself,' said Colonel Johnson doubtfully.

Poirot beamed upon him.

'No, no. It is I who am putting it like that, not *you*! I am pointing out to you that under these conditions – mental strain, physical *malaise* – it is highly probable that dislikes that were before merely mild and disagreements that were trivial might suddenly assume a more serious character. The result of pretending to be a more amiable, a more forgiving, a more high-minded person than one really is, has sooner or later the effect of causing one to behave as a more disagreeable, a more ruthless and an altogether more unpleasant person than is actually the case! If you dam the stream of natural behaviour, *mon ami*, sooner or later the dam bursts and a cataclysm occurs!'

Colonel Johnson looked at him doubtfully.

'Never know when you're serious and when you're pulling my leg,' he grumbled.

Poirot smiled at him.

'I am not serious! Not in the least I am I serious! But all the same, it is true what I say – artificial conditions bring about their natural reaction.'

Colonel Johnson's manservant entered the room.

'Superintendent Sugden on the phone, sir.'

'Right. I'll come.'

With a word of apology the chief constable left the room.

He returned some three minutes later. His face was grave and perturbed.

'Damn it all!' he said. 'Case of murder! On Christmas Eve, too!'

Poirot's eyebrows rose.

'It is that definitely – murder, I mean?'

'Eh? Oh, no other solution possible! Perfectly clear case. Murder – and a brutal murder at that!'

'Who is the victim?'

'Old Simeon Lee. One of the richest men we've got! Made his money in South Africa originally. Gold – no, diamonds, I believe. He sunk an immense fortune in manufacturing some particular gadget of mining machinery. His own invention, I believe. Anyway, it's paid him hand over fist! They say he's a millionaire twice over.'

Poirot said: 'He was well liked, yes?'

Johnson said slowly:

'Don't think any one liked him. Queer sort of chap. He's been an invalid for some years now. I don't know very much about him myself. But of course he is one of the big figures of the county.'

'So this case, it will make a big stir?'

'Yes. I must get over to Longdale as fast as I can.'

He hesitated, looking at his guest. Poirot answered the unspoken question:

'You would like that I should accompany you?'

Johnson said awkwardly:

'Seems a shame to ask you. But, well, you know how it is! Superintendent Sugden is a good man, none better, painstaking, careful, thoroughly sound – but – well, he's not an *imaginative* chap in any way. Should like very much, as you are here, benefit of your advice.'

He halted a little over the end part of his speech, making it somewhat telegraphic in style. Poirot responded quickly.

'I shall be delighted. You can count on me to assist you in any way I can. We must not hurt the feelings of the good superintendent. It will be his case – not mine. I am only the unofficial consultant.'

Colonel Johnson said warmly:

'You're a good fellow, Poirot.'

With those words of commendation, the two men started out.

Jenny Eclair
(contemporary)

Jenny Eclair has been described by the *Daily Mirror* as 'the wildest and wickedest comedian in Britain'. She appears regularly at the Edinburgh Festival, where she won the prestigious Perrier Award in 1995 for her show *Prozac and Tantrums*, which was later a best-selling video. As well as her stand-up comic success, she also co-wrote, with Julie Balloo, the BBC Radio 4 series *On Baby Street* and *Just Juliette*. They have also written a number of plays together, including *The Inconvenience* and *Mrs Nosey Parker*. Jenny Eclair was the first woman to guest-edit the men's magazine *Loaded*. She made her West End debut in Nell Dunn's *Steaming* and has appeared in numerous television shows such as *Jenny Eclair's Private Function*, *Jenny Eclair Squats* and *Edinburgh or Bust*. Her first novel, *A Camberwell Beauty*, was published in 2000.

This extract from *The Book of Bad Behaviour* (1994) gives characteristic Eclair hints on how to make the worst of Christmas.

Christmas is a time of great trauma. Everybody apart from very rich people hate it (they'll give each other Cartier watches and then go skiing, hopefully to somewhere that they'll be engulfed in an avalanche). Every year on Christmas day I like to tell my mother that I'm a lesbian, even though I'm not. It just gets everything going.

The general rule on Christmas day is to start drinking as soon as you have the strength to take the top of the Warninks. It's always better to be a bit pissed whilst opening crap presents because it takes the edge off the disappointment. Christmas started going wrong for me when I was about 14. All I wanted was some clothes, some money, some make-up, some jewellery, some perfume, some platforms, some tights, some electric curlers, a handbag, a leather jacket, a Jackie annual, a selection box, a Pick Of The Pops album featuring a girl on the cover wearing kinky boots full of really bad cover versions, a stereo, a telly for my room and my own front door key. What I actually got was an angle poise lamp so that I didn't strain my eyes whilst I did my homework. My mother ended up with that angle poise lamp – she wore it all Christmas day, tightly wrapped around her neck.

My brother had a 'Christmas face' – basically a sneer as he opened presents which were cheap versions of what he actually wanted. Even now he never opens a gift without asking if you've kept the receipt.

The older I get the more I loathe Christmas, because now I have a horrible family of my own to add to the one which previously scarred me for life.

Xmas means seeing relatives, so a lot of old people who have outlived their savings come round to ponce food off you which they eat with a funny clicking noise. In exchange you get a Christmas present of some second hand cotton buds wrapped up in a bit of Womans Realm.

I can't see the point in making tons of food if people are just going to sit there and eat it. I always buy a Xmas cake from Marks and Spencers which sits in the cupboard looking festive and then is taken back on the 27th and swapped for a new bra.

The way to deal with Christmas of course, is to spoil it so much for everyone that they don't look forward to it next time. Eventually their expectations will be so low that you should be able to get away with spending about £15 on them.

The worst people at Christmas time are the ones that don't spend any money at all, and make everything themselves; cards, wine, food, gifts. Then they chunder on about the true spirit of Christmas which is no excuse for giving you something made out of coat hangers. My mother, in a characteristic demonstration of meanness, once gave all the female members of the family an orange with a load of cloves shoved into it. Apparently this was a pomander and was meant to sweetly scent our knicker drawers which is fine if you like your pants smelling of putrid vegetation. The oranges went mouldy and it took ages to get the spores out of my gussets.

If you can't be bothered to buy anything at all, wrap up something that's been lying around the house for ages; a hair band, a pencil or a cassette head-cleaner. Maybe a flannel and some soap; old bits of soap can look brand new if you wrap them in cling film. Another good trick is to get an old book from a junk shop and forge the author's signature – hey presto! A signed first edition.

I usually go on a very strict diet over Xmas. This makes everyone else who is stuffing themselves feel like they've got food problems. In fact it's me being a complete twat with half a grapefruit that's the problem. Obviously, I don't give up alcohol on my very strict diet. In fact, drinking on an empty stomach is the most efficient way of getting pissed. Basically, I don't like spending my money on food that disappears down other people's necks, so I make sure that everything I cook is so disgusting that people never want to come to my house again. Christmas dinner is easily ruined by under-cooking the turkey by several hours, so that it bleeds dramatically all over the table. I also have a habit of mistaking the bottle of washing-up liquid for brandy and liberally dousing the pudding in lemon squeezy. This has the added fun factor of making people foam at the mouth, whereupon I phone the relevant authorities and have everyone taken away and put in quarantine . . .

Nancy Mitford
(1904–73)

Nancy Mitford was the eldest of Baron Redesdale's family of six daughters and one son. The glamorous and eccentric family was notorious for its politics: Nancy's sister Diana was a fascist who left her husband for Oswald Mosley; Unity became a Nazi who spent time with Adolf Hitler, and Jessica was a Communist, while Nancy herself embraced Socialism. During World War II she worked in London as an air raid precautions volunteer. She was unhappily married and, following an ectopic pregnancy, the result of an affair with a Free French officer, she was unable to have children. As well as her witty novels, such as *The Pursuit of Love* (1945) and *Love in a Cold Climate* (1949), Mitford wrote biographies of Voltaire and Frederick the Great and edited *Noblesse Oblige* (1956), the book in which the controversial 'U' (upper-class) and 'Non-U' classification of linguistic usage and behaviour was established. Mitford fell in love with an older French soldier and lived in Paris for the latter part of her life.

This extract comes from *Christmas Pudding* (1932), a novel that satirises the classic characters who attend an upper-class English country house Christmas, from the dominant dowager to the half-wit uncle and the parasitic freeloaders.

Lady Bobbin was always most particular that the feast of Christmas should be kept by herself, her family and dependents at Compton Bobbin in what she was pleased to call 'good old-fashioned style'. In her mind, always rather a muddled organ, this entailed a fusion of the Christmas customs brought to his adopted country by the late Prince Consort with those which have been invented by the modern Roman-Catholic school of Sussex Humorists in a desperate attempt to revive what they suppose to have been the merrieness of England as it was before she came to be ruled by sour Protestants. And this was odd, because Germans and Roman Catholics were ordinarily regarded by Lady Bobbin with wild abhorrence. Nothing, however, could deter her from being an ardent and convinced Merrie Englander. The maypole on the village green, or more usually, on account of pouring rain, in the village hall; nocturnal expeditions to the local Druid stones to see the sun rise over the Altar Stone, a feat which it was seldom obliging enough to perform; masques in the summer, madrigals in the winter and Morris dances all the year round were organized and led by Lady Bobbin with an energy which might well have been devoted to some better cause. This can be accounted for by the fact of her having a sort of idea that in Merrie England there had been much hunting, no motor cars and that her bugbear, Socialism, was as yet unknown. All of which lent that imaginary period every attribute, in her eyes, of perfection.

But although each season of the year had its own merrie little rite it was at Christmas time that Lady Bobbin and her disciples in the neighbourhood really came into their own, the activities which she promoted during the rest of the year

merely paving the way for an orgy of merrieness at Yule. Her
first step in this direction was annually to summon at least
thirty of the vast clan of Bobbin relations to spend the feast
beneath their ancestral roof, and of these nearly twenty would,
as a rule, find it convenient to obey. The remainder, even if
their absence in Araby or Fair Kashmir rendered it palpably
unlikely that they should accept, were always sent their invi-
tation just the same. This was called Decent Family Feeling.
Having gathered together all those of her late husband's relations who were available to come (her own had mostly died
young from the rigours of tea planting in the Torrid Zone) she
would then proceed to arrange for them to have a jolly
Christmas. In this she was greatly helped by her brother-in-
law, Lord Leamington Spa, who was also a fervent Merrie
Englander, although, poor man, having been banished by
poverty from his country estates and obliged to live all the year
round in Eaton Square, he had but little scope for his activities
in this direction. Those who should have been Lady Bobbin's
prop and mainstay at such a time, her own children, regarded
the whole thing with a sort of mirthful disgust very injurious
to her feelings. Nothing, however, could deter her from her
purpose, and every year at Compton Bobbin the German and
the Sussex customs were made to play their appointed parts.
Thus the Christmas Tree, Christmas stockings and other activities of Santa Claus, and the exchange through the post of
endless cards and calendars (German); the mistletoe and holly
decorations, the turkeys, the boar's head, and a succession of
carol singers and mummers (Sussex Roman Catholic); and
the unlimited opportunity to over-eat on every sort of

unwholesome food washed down with honest beer, which forms the groundwork for both schools of thought, combined to provide the ingredients of Lady Bobbin's Christmas Pudding . . .

Christmas Day itself was organized by Lady Bobbin with the thoroughness and attention to detail of a general leading his army into battle. Not one moment of its enjoyment was left to chance or to the ingenuity of her guests; these received on Christmas Eve their marching orders, orders which must be obeyed to the letter on pain of death. Even Lady Bobbin, however, superwoman though she might be, could not prevent the day from being marked by a good deal of crossness, much overeating, and a series of startling incidents.

The battle opened, as it were, with the Christmas stockings. These, in thickest worsted, bought specially for the occasion, were handed to the guests just before bedtime on Christmas Eve, with instructions that they were to be hung up on their bedposts by means of huge safety pins, which were also distributed. Lady Bobbin and her confederate, Lord Leamington Spa, then allowed a certain time to elapse until, judging that Morpheus would have descended upon the household, they sallied forth together (he arrayed in a white wig, beard and eyebrows and red dressing-gown, she clasping a large basket full of suitable presents) upon a stealthy noctambulation, during the course of which every stocking was neatly filled. The objects thus distributed were exactly the same every year, a curious and wonderful assortment including a pocket handkerchief, Old Moore's Almanack, a balloon not as yet blown up, a mouth organ, a ball of string, a penknife, an instrument for taking stones out of horses' shoes, a book of jokes, a puzzle, and, deep down in the woolly toe of the stocking, whence it would emerge in a rather hairy condition, a chocolate baby. Alas! Most of Lady Bobbin's guests felt that they would willingly have forgone these delightful but inexpensive objects in return for the night's sleep of which they were thus deprived. Forewarned though they were, the shadowy and terrifying appearance of Lord Leamington Spa fumbling about the foot of their beds in the light of a flickering candle gave most of them such a fearful start that all thoughts of sleep were banished for many hours to come.

For the lucky ones who did manage to doze off a rude shock was presently in store. At about five o'clock in the morning Master Christopher Robin Chadlington made a tour of the bedrooms, and having awoken each occupant in turn with a blast of his mouth organ, announced in a voice fraught with tragedy that Auntie Gloria had forgotten to put a chocolate baby in his stocking. 'Please might I have a bit of yours?' This quaint ruse was only too successful, and Christopher Robin acquired thereby no fewer than fourteen chocolate babies, all of which he ate before breakfast. The consequences, which were appalling, took place under the dining-room table at a moment when everybody else was busily opening the Christmas post. After this, weak but cheerful, young Master Chadlington spent the rest of the day in bed practising on his mouth organ.

By luncheon time any feelings of Christmas goodwill which the day and the religious service, duly attended by all, might have been expected to produce had quite evaporated, and towards the end of that meal the dining-room echoed with sounds of furious argument among the grown-ups . . .

The afternoon was so wet and foggy, so extremely unseasonable, in fact, that Lady Bobbin was obliged with the utmost reluctance to abandon the paper chase which she had organized. Until four o'clock, therefore, the house party was left to enjoy in peace that exquisite discomfort which can only be produced by overfed slumberings in arm-chairs. At four punctually everybody assembled in the ballroom while for nearly an hour the Woodford school children mummed. It was the Woodford school children's annual burden to mum at Christmas; it was the annual burden of the inhabitants of Compton Bobbin to watch the mumming. Both sides, however, bore this infliction with fortitude, and no further awkwardness took place until after tea, when Lord Leamington Spa, having donned once more his dressing-gown and wig, was distributing gifts from the laden branches of the Christmas Tree. This was the big moment of the day. The tree, of course, immediately caught fire, but this was quite a usual occurrence, and the butler had no difficulty in putting it out. The real crisis occurred when Lady Bobbin opened the largish, square parcel which had 'To darling mummy from her very loving little Bobby' written on it, and which to Lady Bobbin's rage and horror was found to contain a volume entitled *The Sexual Life of Savages in Northern Melanesia*. This classic had been purchased at great expense by poor Bobby as a present for Paul, and had somehow changed places with *Tally Ho! Songs of Horse and Hound*, which was intended for his mother, and which, unluckily, was a volume of very similar size and shape. Bobby, never losing his head for an instant, explained volubly and in tones of utmost distress to his mother and the company in general that the shop must have sent the wrong book by mistake, and this explanation was rather ungraciously accepted. Greatly to Bobby's disgust, however, *The Sexual Life of Savages in Northern Melanesia* was presently consigned to the stoke-hole flames by Lady Bobbin in person.

The remaining time before dinner, which was early so that the children could come down, was spent by Bobby and Héloïse rushing about the house in a state of wild excitement. Paul suspected, and rightly as it turned out, that this excess of high spirits boded no good to somebody. It was quite obvious to the student of youthful psychology that some practical joke was on hand. He wondered rather nervously where the blow would fall.

It fell during dinner. Captain Chadlington was in the middle of telling Lady Bobbin what the P.M. had said to him about pig-breeding in the West of England when a loud whirring noise was heard under his chair. He looked down, rather startled, turned white to the lips at what he saw, sprang to his feet and said, in a voice of unnatural calm: 'Will the women and children please leave the room immediately. There is an infernal machine under my chair.' A moment of panic ensued. Bobby and Héloïse, almost too swift to apprehend his meaning, rushed to the door shrieking, 'A bomb, a bomb, we shall all be blown up,' while everyone else stood transfixed with horror, looking at the small black box under Captain Chadlington's chair as though uncertain of what they should do next. Paul alone remained perfectly calm. With great presence of mind he advanced towards the box, picked it up and conveyed it to the pantry sink, where he left it with the cold water tap running over it. This golden deed made him, jointly with Captain Chadlington, the hero of the hour. Lady Bobbin shook hands with him and said he was a very plucky young fellow and had saved all their lives, and he was overwhelmed with thanks and praise on every side. Captain Chadlington, too, was supposed to have shown wonderful fortitude in requesting the women and children to leave the room before mentioning his own danger. Only Bobby and Héloïse received no praise from any-body for their behaviour and were, indeed, more or less, sent to Coventry for the rest of the evening.

Captain Chadlington secretly delighted to think that he was now of such importance politically that attempts were made on his life (he never doubted for a moment that this was the doing of Bolshevik agents) went off to telephone to the police. Bobby and Héloïse, listening round the corner, heard him say: 'Hullo, Woodford police? It is Captain Chadlington, M.P., speaking from Compton Bobbin. Look here, officer, there has just been an attempt to assassinate me. The Bolsheviks, I suppose. An infernal machine under my chair at dinner. Would you send somebody along to examine it at once, please, and inform Scotland Yard of what has happened?'

Lady Brenda said: 'I have always been afraid of something like this ever since Charlie made that speech against Bolshevism at Moreton-in-Marsh. Anyhow, we must be thankful that it was no worse.'

Lady Bobbin said that perhaps now the Government would do something about the Bolsheviks at last.

Lord Leamington Spa said that he didn't like it at all, which was quite true, he didn't, because on Christmas night after dinner he always sang 'The Mistletoe Bough' with great feeling and now it looked as though the others would be too busy talking about the bomb to listen to him.

Michael Lewes and Squibby Almanack dared to wonder whether it was really an infernal machine at all, but they only imparted this scepticism to each other.

The duchess said that of course it would be very good publicity for Charlie Chadlington, and she wondered – but added that perhaps, on the whole, he was too stupid to think of such a thing.

Captain Chadlington said that public men must expect this sort of thing and that he didn't mind for himself, but that it was just like those cowardly dagoes to attempt to blow up a parcel of women and children as well.

Everybody agreed that the tutor had behaved admirably.

'Where did you get it from?' Paul asked Bobby, whom he presently found giggling in the schoolroom with the inevitable Héloïse.

'A boy in my house made it for me last half; he says nobody will be able to tell that it's not a genuine bomb. In fact, it is a genuine one, practically, that's the beauty of it. Poor old Charlie Chad., he's most awfully pleased about the whole thing, isn't he, fussing about with those policemen like any old turkey cock. Oh! It all went off too, too beautifully, egI cegouldn't thegink egit fegunnegier, cegould yegou?'

'I think you're an odious child,' said Paul, 'and I've a very good mind to tell your mother about you.'

'That would rather take the gilt off your heroic action, though, wouldn't it, old boy?' said Bobby comfortably.

The local police, as Bobby's friend had truly predicted, were unable to make up their minds as to whether the machine was or was not an infernal one. Until this pretty point should be settled Captain Chadlington was allotted two human bull-dogs who were instructed by Scotland Yard that they must guard his life with their own. A camp bed was immediately made up for one of these trusty fellows in the passage, across the captain's bedroom door, and the other was left to prowl about the house and garden all night, armed to the teeth.

'Darling,' said the Duchess to Bobby, as they went upstairs to bed after this exhausting day, 'have you seen the lovely man who's sleeping just outside my room? I don't know what your mother expects to happen, but one is only made of flesh and blood after all.'

'Well, for goodness sake, try and remember that you're a duchess again now,' said Bobby, kissing his aunt good night.

Janet Hills
(1919–56)

Janet Hills was a film and television critic for *The Times* and its *Educational Supplement*. She was born in Epsom, the daughter of a doctor, but was brought up in the West Country after her family moved to Gloucestershire. She graduated from Somerville College, Oxford, with a degree in English. During World War II she served in the intelligence service and later with the British military government in Berlin. After the war, Hills trained as a teacher, but soon moved into journalism, particularly criticism.

The following story, 'A Surrey Christmas', was found in a collection entitled *Fragments* and published by her family not long after her tragically early death at the age of 36.

Before I give myself over to Christmas good will, I am making a list of the people whom I would like to murder. Every day I collect a few more, and I am knitting their descriptions into a huge purple stocking. I do not know any of their names.

Bypassing milk bottles and cats, I shall go straight to the first human beings up upset my day. At 8.35 a.m. they are waiting for me in the Underground, pressed against the fivepenny ticket machine while they search all their pockets for money. When I have finally dislodged them and put in my sixpence, they lean over my shoulder and insert another so that our change is mingled. By this ruse they beat me to the escalator, where they stand on the left side entertaining their friends, with their elbows sticking out like branches.

In the train they do not quite manage to get seats because rows of sturdy young men in city black are there already, entrenched behind newspapers; but they sweep the weaker passengers away from the straps and the walls. Then they light cigarettes and gesture with them as they talk, thus distracting attention from their sharp-edged suitcases which lie in wait in the middle of the floor. At Paddington, thank goodness, some of them get out and set off to besiege the booking office with detailed questions about times and platforms of trains, while a queue forms and the enquiry office stands empty. Jostling their way to the doors, they ostentatiously trip over my carefully arranged briefcase and bag, and glance at me reproachfully.

Out in the open air again, I wait at the bus stop, mentally working on my stocking. Here the tactics vary. Sometimes my enemies rush past me on the gutter side while I am waiting for my turn to get on, and snarl because I am in their way. At other times, still more diabolically, they stand in front of me, stolidly staring at the bus until I try to pass them, when they become indignantly obstructive. Inside, they refuse to pass along the car and the conductor will not let me travel on the step, so I have to stand on one foot all the way. On the other hand, if by any chance the bus happens to be almost empty, they ignore vacant seats and sink down beside me, breathing heavily and propping parcels against my legs. I am a tolerant person, and I have no objection to passengers who do plain knitting; but cable stitch, with its third needle, is simply aggressive, and people ought to wait till they get home before they turn the heels of socks.

At lunchtime, when I make my harmless way to Oxford Street, my enemies are there, too, walking four abreast with linked arms or plunging headlong out of side streets. Without any warning they stop dead and stare into windows, then glance sideways gloating as I pull up with such skilled swiftness that someone runs into me from behind. When I am in a hurry they move as slowly as treacle from a spoon; but if at last I decide to turn sideways into a shop, they thunder forwards and sweep me off my course, baring their teeth and prodding with umbrellas. I cannot buy a toy unmolested. One of them has got there first, and is asking how all the different brick games work and explaining the tastes of his seven youngest children. As my turn comes, another sidles up and calls over my shoulder: 'Might I just ask a question?' and then, without waiting for an answer, launches into a complaint and has to be led off to the manager. Someone else stands by to buttonhole the assistant on his way back, and no one else will serve me as bricks are very specialized.

The only thing left to me is to eat – and in all the cafés I can see my enemies hunched over 1,000-page novels while they flick cigarette ash into empty coffee cups. So in the end I go to a place with trays and there, just in front of me, is a familiar figure who changes his mind three times as to which is the largest helping of stewed gooseberries and, grabbing backwards, slops my coffee into the saucer while his sleeve brushes through the artificial cream. Meanwhile, rather too close behind me, another one makes clucking noises and shoves with her tray, simply because I am exercising my right as an Englishwoman to make up my mind in my own time.

At the end of the day, of course, the persecutions of travel are reversed; but a new one is added, for I have bought an evening paper, a luxury which my enemies apparently cannot afford. So they all look over my shoulder or stare at the back, and seem quite affronted when I turn a page. Yesterday, being for once paperless, I discovered yet another kind of aggression, for when I happened to glance absent-mindedly at a *Star* just in front, its owner turned round pointedly and spread it out under my eyes – so that I was forced to gaze out of the window for the entire bus ride.

I almost forgot to mention that at the top of my stocking I am knitting a special rib for the income tax authorities. Since, however, I believe in scrupulous justice, I have not yet decided on the exact design – for I am waiting to discover whether it is really the Inspector of Taxes (4th floor, 'D') or the Collector of

Taxes (London, 16th Collection, Entrance 'B') who must be held responsible for the demand so lovingly saved up and timed with such deadly accuracy for the day when I made my first Christmas shopping list.

Selma Lagerlöf
(1858–1940)

Selma Lagerlöf was a novelist, poet, biographer and short-story writer. In 1909 she became the first woman to win the Nobel Prize for Literature, and in 1914, the first woman member of the Swedish Academy. She was a leading figure in the Swedish romantic revival, and her first book, *The Story of Gösta Berling* (1898), which drew on the traditions and legends of her native Värmland, met with great critical acclaim and was made into a film starring Greta Garbo. She wrote many novels for children and adults, including the trilogy *The Ring of the Löwenskölds* and *The Wonderful Adventures of Nils*.

This fable, 'The Legend of the Christmas Rose', was first published in 1910. It is a tale of spiritual redemption, but is comfortably leavened with robust humour, particularly in the depiction of the central character, the fearsome Robber Mother.

Robber Mother, who lived in Robbers' Cave in Göinge forest, went down to the village one day on a begging tour. Robber Father, who was an outlawed man, did not dare to leave the forest, but had to content himself with lying in wait for the wayfarers who ventured within its borders. But at that time travellers were not very plentiful in Southern Skåne. If it so happened that the man had had a few weeks of ill luck with his hunt, his wife would take to the road. She took with her five youngsters, and each youngster wore a ragged leathern suit and birch-bark shoes and bore a sack on his back as long as himself. When Robber Mother stepped inside the door of a cabin, no one dared refuse to give her whatever she demanded; for she was not above coming back the following night and setting fire to the house if she had not been well received. Robber Mother and her brood were worse than a pack of wolves, and many a man felt like running a spear through them; but it was never done, because they all knew that the man stayed up in the forest, and he would have known how to wreak vengeance if anything had happened to the children or the old woman.

Now that Robber Mother went from house to house and begged, she came one day to Övid, which at that time was a cloister. She rang the bell of the cloister gate and asked for food. The watchman let down a small wicket in the gate and handed her six round bread cakes – one for herself and one for each of the five children.

While the mother was standing quietly at the gate, her youngsters were running about. And now one of them came and pulled at her skirt, as a signal that he had discovered something which she ought to come and see, and Robber Mother followed him promptly.

The entire cloister was surrounded by a high and strong wall, but the youngster had managed to find a little back gate which stood ajar. When Robber Mother got there, she pushed the gate open and walked inside without asking leave, as it was her custom to do.

Övid Cloister was managed at that time by Abbot Hans, who knew all about herbs. Just within the cloister wall he had planted a little herb garden, and it was into this that the old woman had forced her way.

At first glance Robber Mother was so astonished that she paused at the gate. It was high summertide, and Abbot Hans' garden was so full of flowers that the eyes were fairly dazzled by the blues, reds, and yellows, as one looked into it. But presently an indulgent smile spread over her features, and she started to walk up a narrow path that lay between many flower-beds.

In the garden a lay brother walked about, pulling up weeds. It was he who had left the door in the wall open, that he might throw the weeds and tares on the rubbish heap outside.

When he saw Robber Mother coming in, with all five youngsters in tow, he ran toward her at once and ordered them away. But the beggar woman walked right on as before. She cast her eyes up and down, looking now at the stiff white lilies which spread near the ground, then on the ivy climbing high upon the cloister wall, and took no notice whatever of the lay brother.

He thought she had not understood him, and wanted to take her by the arm and turn her toward the gate. But when the robber woman saw his purpose, she gave him a look that sent him reeling backward. She had been walking with back bent under her Beggar's pack, but now she straightened herself to her full height. 'I am Robber Mother from Göinge forest; so touch me if you dare!' And it was obvious that she was as certain she would be left in peace as if she had announced that she was the Queen of Denmark.

And yet the lay brother dared to oppose her, although now, when he knew who she was, he spoke reasonably to her, 'You must know, Robber Mother, that this is a monks' cloister, and no woman in the land is allowed within these walls. If you do not go away, the monks will be angry with me because I forgot to close the gate, and perhaps they will drive me away from the cloister and the herb garden.'

But such prayers were wasted on Robber Mother. She walked straight ahead among the little flower-beds and looked at the hyssop with its magenta blossoms, and at the honey-suckles, which were full of deep orange-colored flower clusters.

Then the lay brother knew of no other remedy than to run into the cloister and call for help.

He returned with two stalwart monks, and Robber Mother saw that now it meant business! With feet firmly planted she stood in the path and began shrieking in strident tones all the awful vengeance she would wreak on the cloister if she couldn't remain in the herb garden as long as she wished. But the monks did not see why they need fear her and thought only of driving her out. Then Robber Mother let out a perfect volley of shrieks, and, throwing herself upon the monks, clawed and bit at them; so did all the youngsters. The men soon learned that she could overpower them, and all they could do was to go back into the cloister for reinforcements.

As they ran through the passage-way which led to the cloister, they met Abbot Hans, who came rushing out to learn what all this noise was about.

Then they had to confess that Robber Mother from Göinge forest had come into the cloister and that they were unable to drive her out and must call for assistance.

But Abbot Hans upbraided them for using force and forbade their calling for help. He sent both monks back to their work, and although he was an old and fragile man, he took with him only the lay brother.

When Abbot Hans came out in the garden, Robber Mother was still wandering among the flower-beds. He regarded her with astonishment. He was certain that Robber Mother had never before seen an herb garden; yet she sauntered leisurely between all the small patches, each of which had been planted with its own species of rare flower, and looked at them as if they were old acquaintances. At some she smiled, at others she shook her head.

Abbot Hans loved his herb garden as much as it was possible for him to love anything earthly and perishable. Wild and terrible as the old woman looked, he couldn't help liking that she had fought with three monks for the privilege of viewing the garden in peace. He came up to her and asked in a mild tone if the garden pleased her.

Robber Mother turned defiantly toward Abbot Hans, for she expected only to be trapped and overpowered. But when she noticed his white hair and bent form, she answered peaceably,

'First, when I saw this, I thought I had never seen a prettier garden; but now I see that it can't be compared with one I know of.'

Abbot Hans had certainly expected a different answer. When he heard that Robber Mother had seen a garden more beautiful than his, a faint flush spread over his withered cheek. The lay brother, who was standing close by, immediately began to censure the old woman. 'This is Abbot Hans,' said he, 'who with much care and diligence has gathered the flowers from far and near for his herb garden. We all know that there is not a more beautiful garden to be found in all Skåne, and it is not befitting that you, who live in the wild forest all the year around, should find fault with his work.'

'I don't wish to make myself the judge of either him or you,' said Robber Mother. 'I'm only saying that if you could see the garden of which I am thinking you would uproot all the flowers planted here and cast them away like weeds.'

But the Abbot's assistant was hardly less proud of the flowers than the Abbot himself, and after hearing her remarks he laughed derisively. 'I can understand that you only talk like this to tease us. It must be a pretty garden that you have made for yourself amongst the pines in Göinge forest! I'd be willing to wager my soul's salvation that you have never before been within the walls of an herb garden.'

Robber Mother grew crimson with rage to think that her word was doubted, and she cried out: 'It may be true that until today I had never been within the walls of an herb garden; but you monks, who are holy men, certainly must know that on every Christmas Eve the great Göinge forest is transformed into a beautiful garden, to commemorate the hour of our Lord's birth. We who live in the forest have seen this happen every year. And in that garden I have seen flowers so lovely that I dared not lift my hand to pluck them.'

The lay brother wanted to continue the argument, but Abbot Hans gave him a sign to be silent. For, ever since his childhood, Abbot Hans had heard it said that on every Christmas Eve the forest was dressed in holiday glory. He had often longed to see it, but he had never had the good fortune. Eagerly be begged and implored Robber Mother that he might come up to the Robbers' Cave on Christmas Eve. If she would only send one of her children to show him the way, he could ride up there alone, and he would never betray them – on the contrary, he would reward them, in so far as it lay in his power.

Robber Mother said no at first, for she was thinking of Robber Father and of the peril which might befall him should she permit Abbot Hans to ride up to their cave. At the same time the desire to prove to the monk that the garden which she knew was more beautiful than his got the better of her, and she gave in.

'But more than one follower you cannot take with you,' said she, 'and you are not to waylay us or trap us, as sure as you are a holy man.'

This Abbot Hans promised, and then Robber Mother went her way. Abbot Hans commanded the lay brother not to reveal to a soul that which had been agreed upon. He feared that the monks, should they learn of his purpose, would not allow a man of his years to go up to the Robbers' Cave.

Nor did he himself intend to reveal his project to a human being. And then it happened that Archbishop Absalon from Lund came to Övid and remained through the night. When Abbot Hans was showing him the herb garden, he got to thinking of Robber Mother's visit, and the lay brother, who was at work in the garden, heard Abbot Hans telling the Bishop about Robber Father, who these many years had lived as an outlaw in the forest, and asking him for a letter of ransom for the man, that he might lead an honest life among respectable folk. 'As things are now,' said Abbot Hans, 'his children are growing up into worse malefactors than himself, and you will soon have a whole gang of robbers to deal with up there in the forest.'

But the Archbishop replied that he did not care to let the robber loose among honest folk in the villages. It would be best for all that he remain in the forest.

Then Abbot Hans grew zealous and told the Bishop all about Göinge forest, which, every year at Yuletide, clothed itself in summer bloom around the Robbers' Cave. 'If these bandits are not so bad but that God's glories can be made manifest to them, surely we cannot be too wicked to experience the same blessing.'

The Archbishop knew how to answer Abbot Hans. 'This much I will promise you, Abbot Hans,' he said, smiling, 'that any day you send me a blossom from the garden in Göinge forest, I will give you letters of ransom for all the outlaws you may choose to plead for.'

The lay brother apprehended that Bishop Absalon believed as little in this story of Robber Mother's as he himself; but

Abbot Hans perceived nothing of the sort, but thanked Absalon for his good promise and said that he would surely send him the flower.

Abbot Hans had his way. And the following Christmas Eve he did not sit at home with his monks in Övid Cloister, but was on his way to Göinge forest. One of Robber Mother's wild youngsters ran ahead of him, and close behind him was the lay brother who had talked with Robber Mother in the herb garden.

Abbot Hans had been longing to make this journey, and he was very happy now that it had come to pass. But it was a different matter with the lay brother who accompanied him. Abbot Hans was very dear to him, and he would not willingly have allowed another to attend him and watch over him; but he didn't believe that he should see any Christmas Eve garden. He thought the whole thing a snare which Robber Mother had, with great cunning, laid for Abbot Hans, that he might fall into her husband's clutches.

While Abbot Hans was riding toward the forest, he saw that everywhere they were preparing to celebrate Christmas. In every peasant settlement fires were lighted in the bath-house to warm it for the afternoon bathing. Great hunks of meat and bread were being carried from the larders into the cabins, and from the barns came the men with big sheaves of straw to be strewn over the floors.

As he rode by the little country churches, he observed that each parson, with his sexton, was busily engaged in decorating his church; and when he came to the road which leads to Bösjo Cloister, he observed that all the poor of the parish were coming with armfuls of bread and long candles, which they had received at the cloister gate.

When Abbot Hans saw all these Christmas preparations, his haste increased. He was thinking of the festivities that awaited him, which were greater than any the others would be privileged to enjoy.

But the lay brother whined and fretted when he saw how they were preparing to celebrate Christmas in every humble cottage. He grew more and more anxious, and begged and implored Abbot Hans to turn back and not to throw himself deliberately into the robber's hands.

Abbot Hans went straight ahead, paying no heed to his lamentations. He left the plain behind him and came up into desolate and wild forest regions. Here the road was bad, almost like a stony and burr-strewn path, with neither bridge nor plank to help them over brooklet and rivulet. The farther they rode, the colder it grew, and after a while they came upon snow-covered ground.

It turned out to be a long and hazardous ride through the forest. They climbed steep and slippery side paths, crawled over swamp and marsh, and pushed through windfall and bramble. Just as daylight was waning, the robber boy guided them across a forest meadow, skirted by tall, naked leaf trees and green fir trees. Back of the meadow loomed a mountain wall, and in this wall they saw a door of thick boards. Now Abbot Hans understood that they had arrived, and dismounted. The child opened the heavy door for him, and he looked into a poor mountain grotto, with bare stone walls. Robber Mother was seated before a log fire that burned in the middle of the floor. Alongside the walls were beds of virgin pine and moss, and on one of these beds lay Robber Father asleep.

'Come in, you out there!' shouted Robber Mother without rising, 'and fetch the horses in with you, so they won't be destroyed by the night cold.'

Abbot Hans walked boldly into the cave, and the lay brother followed. Here were wretchedness and poverty! and nothing was done to celebrate Christmas. Robber Mother had neither brewed nor bakes; she had neither washed nor scoured. The youngsters were lying on the floor around a kettle, eating; but no better food was provided for them than a watery gruel.

Robber Mother spoke in a tone as haughty and dictatorial as any well-to-do peasant woman. 'Sit down by the fire and warm yourself, Abbot Hans,' said she, 'and if you have food with you, eat, for the food which we in the forest prepare you wouldn't care to taste. And if you are tired after the long journey, you can lie down on one of these beds to sleep. You needn't be afraid of oversleeping, for I'm sitting here by the fire keeping watch. I shall awaken you in time to see that which you have come up here to see.'

Abbot Hans obeyed Robber Mother and brought forth his food sack; but he was so fatigued after the journey he was hardly able to eat, and as soon as he could stretch himself on the bed, he fell asleep.

The lay brother was also assigned a bed to rest upon, but he didn't dare sleep, as he thought he had better keep his eye on Robber Father to prevent his getting up and capturing Abbot Hans. But gradually fatigue got the better of him, too, and he dropped into a doze.

When he woke up, he saw that Abbot Hans had left his bed and was sitting by the fire talking with Robber Mother. The outlawed robber sat also by the fire. He was a tall, raw-boned man with a dull, sluggish appearance. His back was turned to Abbot Hans, as though he would have it appear that he was not listening to the conversation.

Abbot Hans was telling Robber Mother all about the Christmas preparations he had seen on the journey, reminding her of Christmas feasts and games which she must have known in her youth, when she lived at peace with mankind. 'I'm sorry for your children, who can never run on the village street in holiday dress or tumble in the Christmas straw,' said he.

At first Robber Mother answered in short, gruff sentences, but by degrees she became more subdued and listened more intently. Suddenly Robber Father turned toward Abbot Hans and shook his clenched fist in his face. 'You miserable monk! did you come here to coax from me my wife and children? Don't you know that I am an outlaw and may not leave the forest?'

Abbot Hans looked him fearlessly in the eyes. 'It is my purpose to get a letter of ransom for you from Archbishop Absalon,' said he. He had hardly finished speaking when the robber and his wife burst out laughing. They knew well enough the kind of mercy a forest robber could expect from Bishop Absalon!

'Oh, if I get a letter of ransom from Absalon,' said Robber Father, 'then I'll promise you that never again will I steal so much as a goose.'

The lay brother was annoyed with the robber folk for daring to laugh at Abbot Hans, but on his own account he was well pleased. He had seldom seen the Abbot sitting more peaceful and meek with his monks at Övid than he now sat with this wild robber folk.

Suddenly Robber Mother rose. 'You sit here and talk, Abbot Hans,' she said, 'so that we are forgetting to look at the forest. Now I can hear, even in this cave, how the Christmas bells are ringing.'

The words were barely uttered when they all sprang up and rushed out. But in the forest it was still dark night and bleak winter. The only thing they marked was a distant clang borne on a light south wind.

'How can this bell ringing ever awaken the dead forest?' thought Abbot Hans. For now, as he stood out in the winter darkness, he thought it far more impossible that a summer garden could spring up here than it had seemed to him before.

When the bells had been ringing for a few moments, a sudden illumination penetrated the forest; the next moment it was dark again, and then the light came back. It pushed its way forward between the stark trees, like a shimmering mist. This much it effected: The darkness merged into a faint day-break. Then Abbot Hans saw that the snow had vanished from the ground, as if someone had removed a carpet, and the earth began to take on a green covering. Then the ferns shot up their fronds, rolled like a bishop's staff. The heather that grew on the stony hills and the bog-myrtle rooted in the ground moss dressed themselves quickly in new bloom. The moss-tufts thickened and raised themselves, and the spring blossoms shot upward their swelling buds, which already had a touch of color.

Abbot Hans' heart beat fast as he marked the first signs of the forest's awakening. 'Old man that I am, shall I behold such a miracle?' thought he, and the tears wanted to spring to his eyes. Again it grew so hazy that he feared the darkness would once more cover the earth; but almost immediately there came a new wave of light. It brought with it the splash of rivulet and the rush of cataract. Then the leaves of the trees burst into bloom, as if a swarm of green butterflies came flying and clustered on the branches. It was not only trees and plants that awoke, but crossbeaks hopped from branch to branch, and the woodpeckers hammered on the limbs until the splinters fairly flew around them. A flock of starlings from up country lighted in a fir top to rest. They were paradise starlings. The tips of each tiny feather shone in brilliant reds, and, as the birds moved, they glittered like so many jewels.

Again, all was dark for an instant, but soon there came a new light wave. A fresh, warm south wind blew and scattered over the forest meadow all the little seeds that had been brought from southern lands by birds and ships and winds, and which could not thrive elsewhere because of this country's cruel cold. These took root and sprang up the instant they touched the ground.

When the next warm wind came along, the blueberries and lignon ripened. Cranes and wild geese shrieked in the air, the bullfinches built nests, and the baby squirrels began playing on the branches of the trees.

Everything came so fast now that Abbot Hans could not stop to reflect on how immeasurably great was the miracle that was taking place. He had time only to use his eyes and ears. The next light wave that came rushing in brought with it the scent of newly ploughed acres, and far off in the distance the milkmaids were heard coaxing the cows – and the tinkle of the sheep's bells. Pine and spruce trees were so thickly clothed with red cones that they shone like crimson mantles. The juniper berries changed color every second, and forest flowers covered the ground till it was all red, blue, and yellow. Abbot Hans bent down to the earth and broke off a wild strawberry blossom, and, as he straightened up, the berry ripened in his hand.

The mother fox came out of her lair with a big litter of black-legged young. She went up to Robber Mother and scratched at her skirt, and Robber Mother bent down to her and praised her young. The horned owl, who had just begun his night chase, was astonished at the light and went back to his ravine to perch for the night. The male cuckoo crowed, and his mate stole up to the nests of the little birds with her egg in her mouth.

Robber Mother's youngsters let out perfect shrieks of delight. They stuffed themselves with wild strawberries that hung on the bushes, large as pine cones. One of them played with a litter of young hares; another ran a race with some young crows, which had hopped from their nest before they were really ready; a third caught up an adder from the ground and wound it around his neck and arm.

Robber Father was standing out on a marsh eating raspberries. When he glanced up, a big black bear stood beside him.

Robber Father broke off an osier twig and struck the bear on the nose. 'Keep to your own ground, you!' he said; 'this is my turf.' Then the huge bear turned around and lumbered off in another direction.

New waves of warmth and light kept coming, and now they brought with them seeds from the star-flower. Golden pollen from rye fields fairly flew in the air. Then came butterflies, so big that they looked like flying lilies. The bee-hive in a hollow oak was already so full of honey that it dripped down on the trunk of the tree. Then all the flowers whose seed had been brought from foreign lands began to blossom. The loveliest roses climbed up the mountain wall in a race with the blackberry vines, and from the forest meadow sprang flowers as large as human faces.

Abbot Hans thought of the flower he was to pluck for Bishop Absalon; but each new flower that appeared was more beautiful than the others, and he wanted to choose the most beautiful of all.

Wave upon wave kept coming until the air was so filled with light that it glittered. All the life and beauty and joy of summer smiled on Abbot Hans. He felt that earth could bring no greater happiness than that which welled up about him, and he said to himself, 'I do not know what new beauties the next wave that comes can bring with it.'

But the light kept streaming in, and now it seemed to Abbot Hans that it carried with it something from an infinite distance. He felt a celestial atmosphere enfolding him, and trembling he began to anticipate, now that earth's joys had come, that the glories of heaven were approaching.

Then Abbot Hans marked how all grew still; the birds hushed their songs, the flowers ceased growing, and the young foxes played no more. The glory now nearing was such that the heart wanted to stop beating; the eyes wept without one's knowing it; the soul longed to soar away into the Eternal. From far in the distance faint harp tones were heard, and celestial song, like a soft murmur, reached him.

Abbot Hans clasped his hands and dropped to his knees. His face was radiant with bliss. Never had he dreamed that even in this life it should be granted him to taste the joys of heaven, and to hear angels sing Christmas carols!

But beside Abbot Hans stood the lay brother who had accompanied him. In his mind there were dark thoughts. 'This cannot be a true miracle,' he thought, 'since it is revealed to malefactors. This does not come from God, but has its origin in witchcraft and is sent hither by Satan. It is the Evil One's power that is tempting us and compelling us to see that which has no real existence.'

From afar were heard the sound of angel harps and the tones of a Miserere. But the lay brother thought it was the evil spirits of hell coming closer. 'They would enchant and seduce us,' sighed he, 'and we shall be sold into perdition.'

The angel throng was so near now that Abbot Hans saw their bright forms through the forest branches. The lay brother saw them, too; but back of all this wondrous beauty he saw only some dread evil. For him it was the devil who performed these wonders on the anniversary of our Saviour's birth. It was done simply for the purpose of more effectually deluding poor human beings.

All the while the birds had been circling around the head of Abbot Hans, and they let him take them in his hands. But all the animals were afraid of the lay brother; no bird perched on his shoulder, no snake played at his feet. Then there came a little forest dove. When she marked that the angels were nearing, she plucked up courage and flew down on the lay brother's shoulder and laid her head against his cheek.

Then it appeared to him as if sorcery were come right upon him, to tempt and corrupt him. He struck with his hand at the forest dove and cried in such a loud voice that it rang throughout the forest, 'Go thou back to hell, whence thou art come!'

Just then the angels were so near that Abbot Hans felt the feathery touch of their great wings, and he bowed down to earth in reverent greeting.

But when the lay brother's words sounded, their song was hushed and the holy guests turned in flight. At the same time the light and the mild warmth vanished in unspeakable terror for the darkness and cold in a human heart. Darkness sank over the earth, like a coverlet; frost came, all the growths shrivelled up; the animals and birds hastened away; the rushing of streams was hushed; the leaves dropped from the trees, rustling like rain.

Abbot Hans felt how his heart, which had but lately swelled with bliss, was now contracting with insufferable agony. 'I can never outlive this,' thought he, 'that the angels from heaven had been so close to me and were driven away; that they wanted to sing Christmas carols for me and were driven to flight.'

Then he remembered the flower he had promised Bishop Absalon, and at the last moment he fumbled among the leaves and moss to try and find a blossom. But he sensed how the ground under his fingers froze and how the white snow came gliding over the ground. Then his heart caused him even greater anguish. He could not rise, but fell prostrate on the ground and lay there.

When the robber folk and the lay brother had groped their way back to the cave, they missed Abbot Hans. They took brands with them and went out to search for him. They found him dead upon the coverlet of snow.

Then the lay brother began weeping and lamenting, for he understood that it was he who had killed Abbot Hans because he had dashed from him the cup of happiness which he had been thirsting to drain to its last drop.

When Abbot Hans had been carried down to Övid, those who took charge of the dead saw that he held his right hand locked tight around something which he must have grasped at the moment of death. When they finally got his hand opened, they found that the thing which he had held in such an iron grip was a pair of white root bulbs, which he had torn from among the moss and leaves.

When the lay brother who had accompanied Abbot Hans saw the bulbs, he took them and planted them in Abbot Hans' herb garden.

He guarded them the whole year to see if any flower would spring from them. But in vain he waited through the spring, the summer, and the autumn. Finally, when winter had set in and all the leaves and the flowers were dead, he ceased caring for them.

But when Christmas Eve came again, he was so strongly reminded of Abbot Hans that he wandered out into the garden to think of him. And look! as he came to the spot where he had planted the bare root bulbs, he saw that from them had sprung flourishing green stalks, which bore beautiful flowers with silver white leaves.

He called out all the monks at Övid, and when they saw that this plant bloomed on Christmas Eve, when all the other growths were as if dead, they understood that this flower had in truth been plucked by Abbot Hans from the Christmas garden in Göinge forest. Then the lay brother asked the monks if he might take a few blossoms to Bishop Absalon.

And when he appeared before Bishop Absalon, he gave him the flowers and said: 'Abbot Hans sends you these. They are the flowers he promised to pick for you from the garden in Göinge forest.'

When Bishop Absalon beheld the flowers, which had sprung from the earth in darkest winter, and heard the words, he turned as pale as if he had met a ghost. He sat in silence a moment; thereupon he said, 'Abbot Hans has faithfully kept his word and I shall also keep mine.' And he ordered that a letter of ransom be drawn up for the wild robber who was outlawed and had been forced to live in the forest ever since his youth.

He handed the letter to the lay brother, who departed at once for the Robbers' Cave. When he stepped in there on Christmas Day, the robber came toward him with axe uplifted. 'I'd like to hack you monks into bits, as many as you are!' he said. 'It must be your fault that Göinge forest did not last night dress itself in Christmas bloom.'

'The fault is mine alone,' said the lay brother, 'and I will gladly die for it; but first I must deliver a message from Abbot Hans.' And he drew forth Bishop's letter and told the man that he was free. 'Hereafter you and your children shall play in the Christmas straw and celebrate your Christmas among people, just as Abbot Hans wished to have it,' said he.

Then Robber Father stood there pale and speechless, but Robber Mother said in his name, 'Abbot Hans has indeed kept his word, and Robber Father will keep his.'

When the robber and his wife left the cave, the lay brother moved in and lived all alone in the forest, in constant meditation and prayer that his hard-heartedness might be forgiven him.

But Göinge forest never again celebrated the hour of our Saviour's birth; and of all its glory, there lives today only the plant which Abbot Hans had plucked. It has been named CHRISTMAS ROSE. And each year at Christmastide she sends forth from the earth her green stalks and white blossoms, as if she never could forget that she had once grown in the great Christmas garden at Göinge forest.

christmas at war

And inside the church, packed so tightly together that we could hardly get through, was a crowd so devout, so intent on worship, and absorbed in the beauty of the singing, (once more), of Stille Nacht, *that I, who read my* Times *and know what is happening to the churches of Germany, couldn't believe my eyes.*

ELIZABETH VON ARNIM

Rosa Luxemburg
(1871–1919)

Rosa Luxemburg was born in Zamość, Poland. She became a Communist in 1890 and founded the Polish Social Democratic Party (later the Polish Communist Party). In 1898 she moved to Berlin and became involved in left-wing politics there. When World War I broke out, she formed the Spartacus League with Karl Liebknecht and spent most of the war in prison. They were both murdered during an abortive uprising of 1919.

The following is a letter Luxemburg wrote to Karl's wife, Sonja, who, unlike her husband, was not politically active. Luxemburg addressed some of her most moving letters about prison life to Sonja. In this one she demonstrates the keen intellectual curiosity, compassion, and indomitable enthusiasm for intangible pleasures that kept her alive through the many dark days of her short life. She draws some subtle comparisons between the lives of the oppressed water buffalo that pull the prison carts and the prisoners themselves.

Breslau, mid-December, 1917

. . . It's a year now that Karl's been in Luckau. During the past month, I've thought of this often, and exactly one year ago you were visiting me in Wronke, where you presented me with a beautiful Christmas tree . . . This year I had ordered one. But they brought me a real shabby one, with branches missing – no comparison with the one of last year. I don't know how I will fasten the eight little candles I bought. This will be my third Christmas in jail. But don't you take it too hard; I am as calm and cheerful as ever.

Well, yesterday I thought: how strange that I continually live in a happy state of intoxication for no particular reason. So, for example, I am lying here on a stone-hard mattress in a dark cell, around me the usual quiet of a cemetery; one imagines oneself in the grave. From the window, the reflection of the lantern – which burns all night in front of the prison – is drawn on the ceiling. From time to time, one hears, quite muffled, the distant rattling of a passing train or, from nearby under the window, a sentinel clearing his throat; he is slowly taking a few steps in his heavy boots in order to move his stiff legs. The sand rustles so hopelessly beneath his steps that the whole desolation and inescapability of existence rises from it into the damp, dark night.

There I lie, quiet, alone, wrapped in those manifold black scarves of darkness, boredom, confinement, and winter – and, at the same time, my heart beats with an incomprehensible, unknown inner happiness, as if I were walking over a blooming field in radiant sunshine. And I smile at life in the darkness as if I were aware of some magical secret which might confute the lies, the baseness and the sadness and transform them into sheer brightness and felicity.

And at the same time, I myself am searching for a reason for this happiness. But I find none, and again I must smile at myself. I believe that this mystery is nothing other than life itself; the deep darkness of night is beautiful and soft as velvet if only one looks at it properly. And in the rustling of the moist sand beneath the slow, heavy tread of a sentry, a beautiful little song of life is also singing – if only one knows how to listen properly. In such moments I think of you, and I would so much like to share this magical key with you so that, always, in every situation, you will be able to perceive the beauty and happiness of life, so that you too will live in a state of ecstasy as if you were crossing a multicolored meadow.

Of course, I wouldn't dream of feeding you on asceticism and imaginary joys. I do not begrudge you any real sensuous happiness. I would only like to add to that my own inexhaustible inner cheerfulness, so that I shouldn't worry about you and so that you walk through life in a mantle studded with stars which will protect you from all that is petty, trivial, and frightening . . .

Ach, Sonitschka! I have experienced an acute pain here. In the yard where I walk, military wagons often arrive, packed full with sacks, or old uniforms and shirts often spotted with blood . . . They are unloaded here, passed out in the cells, mended, then reloaded, and delivered to the military. The other day, such a wagon came drawn by water buffaloes rather than horses. This was the first time that I saw these animals up close. They are built sturdier and broader than our oxen, with flat heads, their horns bent flat, their skulls rather resembling the skulls of our own sheep; the buffaloes are completely black with large soft eyes. They come from Rumania, they are trophies of war . . . The soldiers who drive the wagon say that it was a very hard job to catch these wild animals and even more difficult to use them, who were so used to freedom, as beasts of burden. They were beaten frightfully to the point where the words apply to them: 'Woe to the defeated.' . . . About a hundred of these animals are said to be in Breslau alone. Moreover, used to the luxuriant pastures of Rumania, they receive miserable and scant folder. They are mercilessly exploited in dragging all kinds of loads, and so they perish rapidly.

Anyway, a few days ago, a wagon loaded with sacks drove into the prison. The cargo was piled up so high that the buffaloes could not make it over the threshold of the gateway. The attending soldier, a brutal character, began to beat away at the animals with the heavy end of his whip so savagely that the overseer indignantly called him to account 'Don't you have any pity for the animals?' 'No one has any pity for us people either!' he answered with an evil laugh, and fell upon them ever more forcefully . . . Finally, the animals started up and got over the hump, but one of them was bleeding . . . Sonitschka, buffalo hide is proverbial for its thickness and toughness, and it was lacerated. Then, during the unloading, the animals stood completely still, exhausted, and one, the one that was bleeding, all the while looked ahead with an expression on its black face and in its soft black eyes like that of a weeping child. It was exactly the expression of a child who has been severely punished and who does not know why, what for, who does not know how to escape the torment and brutality . . . I stood facing the animal and it looked at me; tears were running from my eyes – they were *his* tears One cannot quiver any more painfully over one's dearest brother's sorrow than I quivered in my impotence over this silent anguish.

How far, how irretrievably lost, are the free, succulent, green pastures of Rumania! How different it was with the sun shining, the wind blowing; how different were the beautiful sounds of birds, the melodious calls of shepherds. And here: this strange weird city, the fusty stable, the nauseating mouldy hay mixed with putrid straw, the strange, horrible people – and the blows, the blood running from the fresh wound . . . Oh! my poor buffalo! My poor beloved brother! We both stand here so powerless and spiritless and are united only in pain, in powerlessness and in longing . . .

Meanwhile, the prisoners bustled busily about the wagon, unloading the heavy sacks and carrying them into the building. The soldier, however stuck both hands into his pockets, strolled across the yard with great strides, smiled and softly whistled a popular song. And the whole glorious war passed in front of my eyes . . . Write quickly, I embrace you, Sonitschka.

Your Rosa

Sonitschka, dearest, in spite of it all, be calm and cheerful. That's life, and that's how one must take it; courageously, intrepidly and smilingly–in spite of it all.

Vera Brittain
(1893–1970)

Vera May Brittain grew up in provincial comfort in the North of England. She won a place at Somerville College, Oxford in 1914, but when war came, abandoned her studies to volunteer as a nurse. She served throughout the war in London, Malta and France. In 1918 she returned to Oxford, having lost her fiancé, her only brother and many friends in the fighting. Her wartime experiences are recorded in *Testament of Youth*, which was published in 1933 and became an immediate best-seller on both sides of the Atlantic. She followed up this vivid and passionate autobiography with two sequels, *Testament of Friendship* (1940) and *Testament of Experience* (1957). Brittain wrote twenty-nine books: novels, poetry and non-fiction, including biography. She was a lifelong pacifist and after the war toured the United States lecturing on pacifism and feminism. She married George Catlin, Professor of Politics at Cornell University, in 1925 and they had two children, one of whom is the English politician Shirley Williams.

In this almost unbearably moving passage from *Testament of Youth*, Brittain describes how she spent Christmas 1915, the day she expected to be reunited with her adored fiancé, Roland.

And, when the final information did come, hurriedly written in pencil on a thin slip of paper torn from his Field Service note-book, it brought the enchanted day still nearer than I had dared to hope.

'Shall be home on leave from 24th Dec.–31st. Land Christmas Day. R.'

Even to the unusual concession of a leave which began on Christmas morning after night-duty the Matron proved amenable, and in the encouraging quietness of the winter's war, with no Loos in prospect, no great push in the west even pos-sible, I dared to glorify my days – or rather my nights – by looking forward. In the pleasant peace of Ward 25, where all the patients, now well on the road to health, slept soundly, the sympathetic Scottish Sister teased me a little for my irrepress-ible excitement.

'I suppose you won't be thinking of going off and getting married? A couple of babies like you!'

It was a new and breath-taking thought, a flame to which Roland's mother – who approved of early marriages and believed that ways and means could be left to look after them-selves far better than the average materialistic parent supposed – added fuel when she hinted mysteriously, on a day off which I spent in Brighton, that *this* time Roland might not be content to leave things as they were ... Suppose, I medi-tated, kneeling in the darkness beside the comforting glow of the stove in the silent ward, that during this leave we *did* marry as suddenly, as, in the last one, we became 'officially' engaged? Of course it would be what the world would call – or did call before the War – a 'foolish' marriage. But now that the War seemed likely to be endless, and the chance of making a 'wise' marriage had become, for most people, so very remote, the world was growing more tolerant. No one – not even my family now, I thought – would hold out against us, even though we hadn't a penny beyond our pay. What if, after all, we did marry thus foolishly? When the War was over we could still go back to Oxford, and learn to be writers – or even lecturers; if we were determined enough about it we could return there, even though – oh, devastating, sweet speculation! – I might have had a baby.

I had never much cared for babies or had anything to do with them; before that time I had always been too ambitious, too much interested in too many projects, to become acutely conscious of a maternal instinct. But on those quiet evenings of night-duty as Christmas approached, I would come, half asleep, as near to praying as I had been at any time, even when Roland first went to France or in the days following Loos.

'Oh, God!' my half-articulate thoughts would run, 'do let us get married and let me have a baby – something that is Roland's very own, something of himself to remember him by if he goes . . . It shan't be a burden to his people or mine for a moment longer than I can help, I promise. I'll go on doing war-work and give it all my pay during the War – and as soon as ever the War's over I'll go back to Oxford and take my Finals so that I can get a job and support it. So *do* let me have a baby, dear God!'

The night before Christmas Eve, I found my ward transformed into the gay semblance of a sixpenny bazaar with Union Jacks, paper streamers, crinkled tissue lampshades and

Christmas texts and greetings, all carried out in staggering shades of orange and vivid scarlet and brilliant green. In the cheerful construction of red paper bags, which I filled with crackers and sweets for the men's Christmas stockings, I found that the hours passed quickly enough. Clipping, and sewing, and opening packets, I imagined him reading the letter that I had written him a few days earlier, making various suggestions for meeting him, if he could only write or wire me beforehand, when the Folkestone train arrived at Victoria, and travelling down with him to Sussex.

'And shall I really see you again, and so soon?' it had concluded. 'And it will be the anniversary of the week which contained another New Year's Eve – and *David Copperfield*, and two unreal and wonderful days, and you standing alone in Trafalgar Square, and thinking of – well, what *were* you thinking of? When we were really both children still, and my connection with any hospital on earth was unthought-of, and your departure for the front merely the adventurous dream of some vaguely distant future date. And life was lived, at any rate for two days, in the Omar Khay-yámesque spirit of

> *Unborn to-morrow and dead yesterday –*
> *Why fret about them if To-day be sweet?*

But we are going to better that – even that – *this* time. Au revoir.'

When I went to her office for my railway-warrant in the morning, the Matron smiled kindly at my bubbling impatience, and reminded me how lucky I was to get leave for Christmas.

At Victoria I inquired what boat trains arrived on Christmas Day, and learnt that there was only one, at 7.30 in the evening. The risk, I decided, of missing him in the winter blackness of a wartime terminus was too great to be worth taking: instead, I would go straight to Brighton next morning and wait for him there.

As Christmas Eve slipped into Christmas Day, I finished tying up the paper bags, and with the Sister filled the men's stockings by the exiguous light of an electric torch. Already I could count, perhaps even on my fingers, the hours that must pass before I should see him. In spite of its tremulous eagerness of anticipation, the night again seemed short; some of the convalescent men wanted to go to early services, and that meant beginning temperatures and pulses at 3 a.m. As I took them I listened to the rain pounding on the tin roof, and wondered whether, since his leave ran from Christmas Eve, he was already on the sea in that wild, stormy darkness. When the men awoke and reached for their stockings, my whole being glowed with exultant benevolence; I delighted in their pleasure over their childish home-made presents because my own mounting joy made me feel in harmony with all creation.

At eight o'clock, as the passages were lengthy and many of the men were lame, I went along to help them to the communion service in the chapel of the college. It was two or three years since I had been to such a service, but it seemed appropriate that I should be there, for I felt, wrought up as I was to a high pitch of nervous emotion, that I ought to thank whatever God might exist for the supreme gift of Roland and the love that had arisen so swiftly between us. The music of the organ was so sweet, the sight of the wounded men who knelt and stood with such difficulty so moving, the conflict of joy and gratitude, pity and sorry in my mind so poignant, that tears sprang to my eyes, dimming the chapel walls and the words that encircled them: 'I am the Resurrection and the Life: he that believeth in Me, though he were dead, yet shall he live: and whosoever liveth and believeth in Me shall never die.'

Directly after breakfast, sent on my way by exuberant good wishes from Betty and Marjorie and many of the others, I went down to Brighton. All day I waited there for a telephone message or a telegram, sitting drowsily in the lounge of the Grand Hotel, or walking up and down the promenade, watching the grey sea tossing rough with white surf-crested waves, and wondering still what kind of crossing he had had or was having.

When, by ten o'clock at night, no news had come, I concluded that the complications of telegraph and telephone on a combined Sunday and Christmas Day had made communication impossible. So, unable to fight sleep any longer after a night and a day of wakefulness, I went to bed a little disappointed, but still unperturbed. Roland's family, at their Keymer cottage, kept an even longer vigil; they sat up till nearly midnight over their Christmas dinner in the hope that he would join them, and, in their dramatic, impulsive fashion, they drank a toast to the Dead.

The next morning I had just finished dressing, and was putting the final touches to the pastel-blue crêpe-de-Chine blouse, when the expected message came to say that I was wanted on the telephone. Believing that I was at last to hear the voice for which I had waited for twenty-four hours, I dashed joyously into the corridor. But the message was not from Roland but from Clare; it was not to say that he had arrived home that morning, but to tell me that he had died of wounds at a Casualty Clearing Station on December 23rd.

Tsarina Alexandra Feodorovna (1872–1918)

Alexandra Feodorovna was a German princess, the daughter of Grand Duke Louis of Hesse-Darmstadt and Queen Victoria's daughter, Alice Maud Mary. She became Empress of Russia as the wife of Tsar Nicholas II, whom she married in 1894. She was deeply religious and superstitious and fell under the spell of controversial 'holy man' Rasputin. Alexandra ruled Russia incompetently during her husband's absence at the front during World War I; and when the revolution broke out she was imprisoned by the Bolsheviks with the rest of her family and executed in a cellar at Ekaterinberg in 1918. The relationship between Alexandra and her husband was intensely affectionate, as their correspondence shows. This letter, written during his time with the Russian troops, shows how dearly the royal couple loved one another after 21 years of marriage. The letter was among a trove discovered in a black box in the last prison of the imperial family.

Dec. 30-th 1915

My very own beloved One,

Off you go again alone & its with a very heavy heart I part from you. No more kisses & tender caresses for ever so long – I want to bury myself into you, hold you tight in my arms, make you feel the intense love of mine. You are my very life Sweetheart, and every separation gives such endless heartache – a tearingaway from one, what is dearest & holiest to one. God grant it's not for long – others would no doubt find me foolish & sentimental – but I feel too deeply & intently & my love is fathomlessly deep, Lovebird! – And knowing all your heart carries, anxieties, worries, – so much that is serious, such heavy responsibilities wh. I long to share with you & take the weight upon my shoulders. One prays & again with hope & trust & patience the good will come in due time & you & our country be recompensed for all the heartache & blood-shed. All that have been taken »& burn as candles before God's throne« are praying for victory & success – & where the right cause is, will final victory be! One longs just a bit quicker for some very good news to quieten the restless minds here, to put their small faith to shame. – we have not seen each other quiet-ly this time, alone only ¾ of an hour on Xmas Eve, & yesterday ½ an hour – in bed one cannot speak, too awfully late always, & in the morning no time – so that this visit has flown by, & then the Xmastrees took you away daily – but I am grateful that you came, not counting our joy, your sweet presence delighted several thousands who saw you here. The new year does not count – but, still not to begin it together for the first time since

21 years is still a bit sad. – This letter I fear sounds grumbly, but indeed its not meant to be so, only the heart is very heavy & your loneliness is a source of trouble to me. Others, who are less accustomed to family life, feel such separations far less. – Tho' the heart is engaged, I'll still come to see you off and then go into Church & seek strenght there, & pray for your journey & victory. –

Goodbye my Angel, Husband of my heart I envy my flowers that will accompany you. I press you tightly to my breast, kiss every sweet place with gentle tender love, I, your ownlittle woman, to whom you are All in this world. God bless & protect you, guard you from all harm, guide you safely & firmly into the new year. May it bring glory & sure peace, & the reward for all this war has cost you. I gently press my lips to yours & try to forget everything, gazing into your lovely eyes – I lay on your precious breast, rested my tired head upon it still. This morning I tried to gain calm & strenght for the separation. Goodbye wee one, Lovebird, Sunshine, Huzy mine, Own!

Ever your unto death wife and friend.

( ) a big kiss imprinted here

Sunny.

Elizabeth von Arnim (Countess Mary Annette Beauchamp Russell) (1866–1941)

Elizabeth von Arnim was born Elizabeth Alice Cholmondeley in Sydney, Australia, a cousin of the New Zealand writer Katherine Mansfield, but moved to London while still a child. She married a German count, Henning August von Arnim-Schlagenthin in 1891 and after his death in 1910 (he was 25 years her senior) she settled in Switzerland with her four children, frequently welcoming literary friends such as H. G. Wells and Hugh Walpole. She moved back to London and married Lord Francis Russell. Her best-loved work, *Elizabeth and Her German Garden*, is an autobiographical novel set in her first husband's ancestral land of Pomerania, between Poland and Germany. It was originally published anonymously and, like her later novels, *The Pastor's Wife* and *Mr Skeffington*, the book became enormously popular. The writer adopted the name of her literary alter ego, 'Elizabeth'. Her witty, original style was also critically acclaimed.

'Christmas in a Bavarian Village', published here for the first time, describes the return of the protagonist to a German village Christmas after many years away.

When I got out of the train in the dusk of a dove-coloured afternoon, my daughter ran along the platform to meet me, and with her ran a young man in short leather breeches with bare knees, and it being almost dark, and the costume familiar, I thought it was her husband. So that I greeted him with the proper enthusiasm, seizing his hands in both mine, and crying, 'How charming of you to come out in all the cold!'

Fortunately my son-in-law and I do not kiss, but except for that all was enthusiasm, including, of course, the familiar *Du*.

My daughter pulled my arm. 'It's the taxi-man,' she whispered, struggling to suppress her giggles.

The young man, I must say, let my behaviour wash over him with dignity. Perhaps he thought it was the way all foreigners arrived at stations, and that, far from being a cold race, the English were red hot.

A little subdued, I was led out of the station into a world of Christmas trees. In front of most of the houses stood a tree lit by electric light, and in the middle of the one wide street was a huge one, a pyramid of solemn radiance.

I felt as if I had walked into a Christmas card, – glittering snow, steep-roofed old houses, and the complete windlessness, too, of a Christmas card. Not since 1909 had I had a German Christmas, the last of a string of them, and seeing that 1909 is a long while ago, and that many things have happened since, it was odd how much at home I felt, how familiar everything seemed, and how easily this might have been the Christmas, following in its due order, of 1910.

On the doorstep of the little house in the middle of snow-fields and ringed round with towering mountains, stood, full welcome, my real son-in-law. He was dressed exactly like the taxi-man, in leather shorts and an embroidered shirt, so how could anybody be expected to know which was which? Carefully I looked at him, though embarking, this time, on warmth. 'How charming of you,' I cried, when thoroughly certain, 'to come out in all the cold!' – for I have not many German sentences and the same has to do several times.

Not only was he on the doorstep, but many enchanting smells, very beautiful to the hungry, were there, too, smells of *Leberkuchen*, *Leberwurst*, red cabbage, roasting goose, and the more serious smell, serious because it also attends funerals and envelops mausoleums, of the fir tree standing ready to be lit in the drawing-room.

This was Christmas Eve, the day the Germans, in the evening, celebrate; and while I was taking off my things upstairs, the candles on the tree were lit, so that when I came down the household, consisting of father, mother, small daughter, three white-capped and white-cotton-gloved maids, and two Scotties, were waiting for me in the hall before the shut door of the room of mysteries.

To the strains of *Stille Nacht, heilige Nacht*, we marched in according to age, beginning with the youngest and ending, after me, with the cook. Since, for sometime past, everybody seems to be younger than I am, I was quite pleased about the cook.

I knew exactly what I would find inside the room, for had I not for years myself arranged such rooms with their tree and tables of presents? There were the tables in a familiar row, one for each person, piled with parcels tied up in gay paper and silver ribbon, decorated with pots of cyclamen and azaleas, and there was the tree, with the little *crèche* at its feet, and marzipan sheep flocking round chocolate Wise Men.

We stood in a semicircle, keeping our eyes fixed on the tree and not letting them wander to the tables, because that wouldn't have been manners, and while we were busy singing *Stille Nacht* to the accompanying gramophone, the Scotties, who had no manners, before our outraged eyes ate, one after the other, all the marzipan sheep. Because of custom we couldn't do anything but stand stiff and sing. Both tradition and decency rooted us in immobility. Luckily there were only two verses, and the Wise Men were saved in the nick of time and I thought only Germans could be as disciplined as that, and able by training to appear absorbed in holy words while their hearts must be boiling within them.

But the conduct of the Scotties delayed us in getting to our tables. They had to be dealt with and banished before we were able to turn our attention to joy. Those dogs didn't care a bit that they were disgraced. Inside them, safely tucked away, were the sheep, and I could have sworn they laughed as they were led away.

Slightly subdued – this was the second time I had been subdued – for it seemed a sad thing for the family to lose so many sheep, bought, I knew, this Christmas all fresh and new for me, and destined to appear at least at five Christmases more, I began undoing my parcels, and soon we all got worked up to the proper spirit again. From each table came cries of excitement and joy. From each table somebody was rushing continually to thank and hug, or thank and kiss the hand of somebody else. Even the cook and myself, the *doyennes* of the party, were ready to hug. She luckily, had soon to withdraw to the kitchen, to give the finishing touches to the goose, or I don't know but what we too mightn't have ended in each other's arms.

Wading through torn paper and silver ribbon we went in to dinner, drank, made speeches, and were merry. After dinner we waded back, again, and were less merry and after we had eaten *Baumkuchen* and drunk hot spiced wine we were hardly merry at all, because we would have liked, but couldn't because of tradition and decency, to go to sleep.

'It's impossible,' I said, shaking myself free of the stupor slowly bearing me down, 'to imagine this Germany is any different from the Germany I knew.'

'Oh, but it is –' began my daughter, instantly to be stopped by her husband with a quick, 'Take care –', for one of the maids had come into the room.

This woke me up completely. Take care? What of?

Slightly subdued, for the third time, I allowed myself to be put into my fur coat, and driven to midnight mass. A glittering night. A night of peace and beauty. The bells of the old church on the hill were ringing, and streams of dark figures – *streams*, I noted with astonishment – piously silent, were flowing up towards it. Down in the street the huge Christmas tree stood radiant. On each grave in the churchyard a tiny one burnt, lighting up the whole place with symbols of remembrance and love. And inside the church, packed so tightly together that we could hardly get through, was a crowd so devout, so intent on worship, and absorbed in the beauty of the singing, (once more), of *Stille Nacht*, that I, who read my *Times* and know what is happening to the churches of Germany, couldn't believe my eyes.

'But –' I began, as I hung on to my son-in-law's arm.

'Take care,' he quickly whispered gripping my hand.

Take care. Again. Must one then for ever take so much care? And, after all, what had I said except 'But'?

Kathleen Hersom
(1911–)

Kathleen Hersom was born in Nottingham and by 1939 was for the second time headmistress of a nursery school. At the time of the *Kindertransports* from Germany she sponsored a Jewish girl aged 12, who lived with her through much of the war. Towards its end she volunteered for relief work in Germany, where she witnessed the events she describes in the following story, 'The Christmas Present'. In 1947 she married a colleague from the relief team, and settled in County Durham. When her four children had grown up she revived her earlier interest in writing for young people, and between 1977 and 1989 had six books accepted for publication. Her other titles include *Johnny Oswaldtwistle* (1977), *Maybe it's a Tiger* (1981), *The Spitting Image* (1982), *Johnny Reed's Cat and Other Northern tales* (1987), *The Copycat*, with Donald Hersom (1990), *The Half Child* (1990) and *Listen All of You!* (1990).

I thought there could be nothing easier than writing a Christmas story. There would be no need to rack my brains for a plot, or struggle to create life-like characters. I would simply put down on paper that story which floats into my head each year during the second half of December. It comes as regularly as the mince pies and the plum pudding and the carols. For years I had intended writing it down. Once I put my hand to the pen, I was sure there would be no trouble.

So I rollicked away into the first paragraph, describing a horde of children plodging through the snow in a deep forest; six inches deep, at least, that snow was, and the children, muffled from top to toe, cherry-nosed and eyes shining, were carrying lanterns. Branches heavy with snow bent down to touch them, and a million stars sparkled in the frosty sky. It was almost midnight, and I think the bells were ringing. They made their way to the little church conveniently situated in a forest clearing, where midnight mass was to be celebrated. Just like the Christmas cards it was, the roof smothered in deep snow overhanging into icicles, the dark trees behind it, light piercing from the windows, and small footprints smudging through the snow up to its door. The children left their lanterns and their snowballs in the porch and hurried inside, almost filling the church. A few small square women sat at the back, their heads swathed in white medieval-looking wimples. A tiny boy swung a censer, a while a great genial priest loomed over him. And through the little window above the altar one big star outshone all the rest.

When the mass was over and the children had crossed themselves for the last time, they picked up their lanterns and tugged me by the hand to the little wooden house in the forest where they all lived together, and where they had invited me to a party that was to start at three o'clock in the morning.

Their home inside was scrubbed and neat, and all the rafters and most of the walls were covered with sweet-smelling fir-branches; gingerbread-men and star biscuits hung from the beams, and there were red and white decorations, and flags. Trestle-tables set for some kind of feast were on three sides of the room, and everywhere there was bustle and activity, something like one of those pictures by Breughel, but not so much food.

Here I broke off to read back what I had written so far. The way I had written it made me feel uncomfortable. Where on earth had all this phoney icing-sugar fantasy come from? Was it a nostalgic travesty of the Grimms' fairy stories that had been told to me so often in childhood, translated, perhaps, into a more recent Disneyism? I had intended surging on to the end before making any alterations, but now I felt compelled to go back and get my feet planted firmly on the ground before drowning in a sea of whimsy, and take out all that Snow Whiteish stuff straight away.

But that wasn't easy. Implausible it might be, but could it be called phoney once I accepted that, after all, it wasn't fiction I was writing? It wasn't fiction because it had all really happened and I had been at the party myself, and in that snow, and at the church, so I knew every word was authentic.

The forest I had described was the Duisburger Wald; a great welcome stretch of green in the industrial Ruhr valley. The time was the night of December 24–25, 1946. The children carrying their lanterns through the snow were all Displaced Persons, lost Polish children who had become separated from their parents during the course of the war, or in the confusion and upheaval that followed the ending of it. They did not live in the usual prefabricated sprawl of D.P. camps that littered Germany at that time, but in a small wooden chalet that had once been used for some week-end forestry activity by the Hitler Youth. With them were a few Polish women separated from their own families, all looked after by a kindly house-mother.

I had described them, accurately enough, as 'muffled from head to toe': army greatcoats cut down to size (or, more often, not cut down to size) are all-enveloping. Even an old battledress will reach to the toes provided you are small enough to start with. And whose nose would not be red on a night as cold as that one was? Torches might have been more likely than those over-picturesque Dickensian lanterns, but batteries were unobtainable, so it was lanterns that lighted them through the forest to the midnight mass – though I never learned how they came by those lanterns. The D.P.s had a wonderful knack of 'organizing' things, especially for celebrations. The exuberance of snow and frost and icicles was no Christmas-card make-believe, but just as I said. Old meteorological records somewhere would bear me out. True, I hadn't actually counted the stars, but I remember looking up and thinking that a million was about what it looked like. I could cut out the ringing bells in my final draft. I think they really were there, but so many bells had been melted down for the German war effort that they might just possibly have been a wishfully imagined recollection.

I moved on to what I had written about the midnight mass. Not being a Catholic I was wary of much detailed description here for fear of missing the right significances, but I firmly crossed out that great star looking through the window. Even in 1946 I thought it too trite and dramatic to be true – although it really was there. I let the incense stay, although I remember now that it too had been unobtainable at the time – that jovial Santa-Claus-cum-Friar-Tuck-like-priest was an unscrupulous old bounder when it came to obtaining the unobtainable – and I liked the smell. Good smells were important in those hungry days when the smell of watery turnip soup seeped out of every kitchen, and the stink of corruption hung around the uncleared rubble that stretched for scores of miles beyond the forest.

I carried on with my story, reporting, not imagining, that three-o'clock-in-the-morning party where I had been a guest.

'The children who were too young to have been to mass had been shaken awake and carried in, wrapped in grey army blankets, to blink at the precious candles – candles whose burning was so carefully rationed and conserved – and to poke inquisitive hopeful fingers at the one-inch squares of chocolate set singly at each place. It was good that on this occasion at least, it would not be syphoned off on to the black market.

'The party was a double celebration: not only for Christmas, but for the reunion of one of the Polish women with her children from whom she had been separated for more than four years. Her sixteen-year-old daughter, trailing a small staircase of younger brothers and sisters, had somehow floundered her way across Germany from the east, without documents, and although transport had been almost *non-existent. They had arrived eventually, on this Christmas Eve, at this small Polish barrack in the Duisburger Wald, where, unknown to them, their mother was living.'*

How the red tape of occupying armies, the regulations of Military government and its Control Commission, the ministrations of the Red Cross and UNRRA had been dodged or overcome, or just ignored, I cannot now remember, if I ever heard. Nor did I know how long they had been on their way. That did not matter. With a good map of Germany and Poland, and reference to a history of the Second World War, I might lapse into real fiction here. This is where I might start imagining some of the dangers, narrow escapes, blind eyes and helping hands that there must have been on their road. There could certainly be more than just one story here.

It was, indeed, a well of material to draw on for stories; a remarkable, courageous journey, but not without parallel. I had read articles about similar triumphs written shortly after the war, and I saw a film once that reminded me of it. But never since that night have I been asked to believe such an audacious coincidence as those real children's dramatic entry on Christmas Eve, spotlighted against the background of evergreens and snow and frost and red and white paper flowers and makeshift Polish flags. No short story could hold it.

I was sure that no editor nowadays would find that absurdly neat old-fashioned happy ending acceptable. It was so unlikely that Stanislava and the other children would find their mother at all, but to find her on Christmas Eve of all the three hundred and sixty -five possible days was timing that was far too contrived to be credible – how could I convince anyone that it was not 'contrived' because there was not a single invention in it? Improbable facts make impossible fiction.

Perhaps as a *story* it would be better if I could postpone their arrival till the spring. It would be years before all the Poles would be able to leave Germany. There was no hurry. Spring would thaw out all that excessive snow and frost, and extinguish the spluttering candles and the lanterns at one stroke. There would be no need or reason for the midnight mass. It would perhaps be better artistically that way, as well as easier to believe.

But I braked again. That wouldn't be a Christmas story any more, and it was a Christmas story I was supposed to be writing. A story that wasn't a Christmas story would have no place in this book.

So that is where I left my Christmas story, with that celebration party of a displaced family in the heart of a German forest; with bright beady eyes in Slavonic faces watching a mother enjoying the best Christmas present she could ever wish to have. The facts are so improbable that it would certainly have made impossible fiction. But that doesn't matter, because, as I said before, it is not fiction that I have been writing, whatever the editor, or the readers and I were expecting. The 'story' that floats into my head every Christmas really happened, nearly forty years ago, just exactly as I have written it.

Call it reminiscence, or even history, if you must have a label. It is certainly not fiction.

christmas
romance

'I'm afraid I've got nothing for you,' she apologised to Bernardo. *'Oh, yes you have, my precious little pot-pourri,'* he said huskily. *'You have everything I could possibly desire.'* She was getting rather fond of him. For one thing, he seemed terribly easy to please.

CLARE BOYLAN

Kathleen Norcross
(1928–)

Kathleen Norcross was born in West Riding in Yorkshire, a town that made its living by turning rags into new cloth. Its motto was *inutile ex arte utile* and it boasted a grammar school founded in 1735, which Norcross attended. While reading English at Oxford University, she met the medical student she later married and with whom she spent a memorable year in Manhattan. Now, following her husband's death, she is once more in Oxfordshire. Her first book, *Grass in the Wall*, was published in 1987. 'Poem for Christmas Day' appeared in her collection *A Blue Harvester Mug*.

These are the Christmas joys I wish for you:
Sacrament, first, to greet the new-born Word;
Red sky and robins; noon an egg-shell blue;
At least one moment, when the air is stirred
By angels' wings; at least tuthree gifts . . .
But these, like bulbs one plants, and does not say,
Whose stems stand hidden, in the frozen drifts,
Shall be my secret, love, till Christmas Day.

Cora Sandel (Sara Fabricius)
(1880–1974)

Cora Sandel was born in Oslo. She studied to be a painter, mainly in Paris, but at the age of 40 gave up painting, settled in Sweden with her husband and turned her attention to writing, publishing the first volume of her acclaimed *Alberta* trilogy in 1926. Her complete works, comprising novels, novellas and short stories, were published in six volumes in 1952. Her work is often humorous, but she records human relationships with sympathy as well as irony. This story, 'Artist's Christmas', was written in the late 1920s.

The daylight comes creeping in, stone grey, spreading slowly inside the studio, bringing out of the darkness, as if by magic, frozen windows, a cold stove, a dead world.

Both of them open their eyes simultaneously, each seeing the other's face at the same moment, the slightly haggard and sunken, dogged and tense expression that comes of cold, sleeplessness and inadequate nourishment. 'Come here and get warm,' he says softly.

Silently she moves in under his blanket. 'Christ!' he exclaims, when he feels how cold she is.

Shivering she curls up in the crook of his arm. A tear appears from under her eyelid, travels across her nose and falls heavily on his shirt-sleeve. 'There, there, there,' he murmurs. She gives in and cries helplessly, her face against his neck.

The water is frozen in the bucket, the ink in the ink-well. The panes in the windows and skylight are covered with frost patterns. He wanders about, noting it, while he buttons up his clothes and turns up his collar, trembling with cold. And he pauses in front of the still-life motif, where the flowers are hanging black and rotten and the leeks are lying like corpses. 'Look at this!' he calls out. 'All of it ruined. The jug's cracked from top to bottom. I shan't get anything more out of *that* picture.'

'We should have emptied it,' she remarks from the bed. 'We should have thought of that when it got so much colder last night. The flowers wouldn't have survived anyway.'

'Oh, one always knows what should have been done when

it's too late. Well, well . . . you stay there till the water's boiled for the tea.'

She curls up in the little patch of warmth left in the bed by their two bodies, listening to him hacking a hole in the ice in the bucket and tapping the bottom of the tea-caddy to find the last leaves. 'Good thing we've got some paraffin,' he mutters.

She lies with her eyes closed. She can think no further ahead than to tea, hot tea. The slight whisper of the flame reaches her like a reminder of a better world, a world fit to live in. When you listen to it and lie completely still so that none of the accumulated warmth escapes, it is almost cosy.

He is poking at the stove, raking out the ashes, blowing on his fingers and poking it again; unpleasant sounds that bother her. What's the use of making them today when they haven't so much as a shaving to kindle a fire with?

Then the sound of wood snapping. She half sits up in surprise. He is standing breaking a canvas frame in pieces against his knee. 'I'll light it as soon as you get up,' he says in explanation. 'Then you can get dressed over here by the stove. It's better than nothing.'

A warm wave of gratitude overwhelms her. A frame is no small sacrifice. 'Wonderful!' she cries in excitement. 'Then we'll have our tea in front of the stove.'

The tea warms so that it hurts the spine, the frame burns brightly. It lasts no longer than one might expect, just a few hectic minutes. Cup in hand they squat, turning their bodies so as to feel the warmth all over, greedily taking advantage of every last bit of heat from the embers and ashes. And then the chill is back again, making their faces pinched and grey.

On top of all her other clothes she is wearing his raincoat, over her stockings men's socks, and then wooden clogs. This uniform has come about of itself as the days have passed, cold and penniless. His clothes are ill-fitting and insufficient, the way clothes look when there is too much underneath them. He moves in them stiffly and laboriously.

The rotting floor is just high enough to leave room for the rats; the studio is built virtually on the bare earth. In spring, summer and autumn it is an idyllic spot, the light falling on it attractively, ivy creeping in through cracks and openings. Artists and aesthetes are enraptured at the sight.

But then the winter comes. It turns mouldy and damp. The snow and the rain drip in, there are draughts from every direction, the stove with its crooked, dangerous tin chimney struggles vainly against it all. Sometimes it gives up and stands there cold and dead. Even the frost penetrates the walls and joins them indoors.

All in all one of those incredible dwellings, in fact condemned, which only artists and tramps can consider living in, and then only in Paris. Artists believe they can live anywhere as long as the rent is low and the lighting is good. They bribe the concierge and furtively move a couple of rickety iron bedsteads or a worn-out divan up to the attic. They have to live in misery for a long time before admitting to themselves and to others that they do so.

These two admit they are miserable. Things have reached that point. As recently as yesterday she made the beds and carried out the small daily rites that symbolize hearth and home, washing the dishes, dusting. Today she is doing nothing. With her hands thrust into her sleeves and her head down inside her coat collar, her eyes closed and her feet drawn up under her, she sits on his tall painting-stool cowering like a sick bird.

He tramps around, now and again giving her a pat on the back in passing, before leaving her again. His attitude and expression are those of a malefactor. Their breath comes out of their mouths like smoke.

'You mustn't sit like this,' he says finally. 'It's dangerous. We must go out and take a brisk walk.'

'I haven't the energy. We walked all yesterday, we walked the day before yesterday.'

'Don't exaggerate. We sat for hours in the Louvre yesterday. We sat in St Germain des Prés as well. We're not the only ones to spend our time in churches and museums in this cold.'

She does not reply, merely crouching down farther. Her courage has vanished with the fire that has burnt out and died. She coughs.

Then he takes her by the arm, forces her down from the stool, and says angrily, 'You'll be good enough to come this minute. They'll have to give us another day's credit at the corner. They can't let us perish. Here are your shoes.'

He helps her on with them roughly, with some exasperation. But he puts her feet under his vest while he sits on his haunches and blows into her shoes to warm them, then leads her across to the door. 'You keep the coat on.'

'Are you mad?' She is roused at once from her torpor, turns energetic, gets him to put on the coat, and they hurry out. The rent has been owing for a long time, and just as they are about to walk quickly and carelessly past the concierge, they are caught. A telegraph messenger is standing inside: the telegram is for them.

He signs for it with trembling hands and opens it. His pictures are on exhibition at home in Norway, and he has given that fact as a guarantee. The concierge watches him expectantly. The telegram says: A MERRY CHRISTMAS FROM ALL OF US.

He stuffs it in his pocket with a crooked little smile.

'Nothing of importance, monsieur?'

'Nothing of importance, madame.'

A biting wind drives them along the ice-packed pavement, carrying them with it as it carries paper, trash, withered leaves and other lifeless objects. They stumble in through the swing-door on the corner. The transition to the dense, stifling atmosphere indoors is so extreme that it is painful at first. It takes their breath away. Only gradually do they feel relief. And then it's all marvellous: the tobacco-smoke, the steaming coffee, the babble of voices, the clatter of coins and of checkers. Stifling, enclosed, unhealthy and marvellous. They are seized by a primitive need for shelter, a primeval longing to be together with other living beings, to share their warmth.

Only yesterday it had tortured her to see him pushing through the crowd at the counter, asking for credit yet again. Today she has only one thought: to be allowed to stay.

Squashed into a corner at a small table, people coming and going all about her, the swing-door incessantly bringing in more frozen souls, she has only one idea: to defend her place to the death. When a steaming *café au lait* is put down in front of her she almost grasps the waiter's hand in gratitude.

They drink greedily and broodingly, reminding each other at intervals that they must not do so too fast. You can't sit for long over an empty cup on credit, not on a day like this. But immediately they are drinking again, unable to stop. They watch the colour rise, sudden and intense, in each other's faces, watch their eyes widen and shine. 'Better?' he asks. And he smiles.

He takes out the telegram. It's from her relatives. 'Did you remember that it was Christmas Eve?' he asks.

'Nobody forgets Christmas Eve,' she answers.

He puts his hand over hers. 'I'm going to find you something. We're going to have food and warmth before the evening, if I have to . . .'

He doesn't finish. She says nothing. For a moment she waits, for the usual assurance that money *could* come in the course of the day, he could have sold something at home, the devil take them all if he hadn't. The assurance is not made. So he's thinking of begging again from his friends at the Dôme, going from table to table, explaining, giving assurances.

She draws her hand away and places it over his. 'Shall we try to manage one day more? On Christmas Eve the churches are open till midnight.'

He shakes his head obstinately.

*

Towards evening she is sitting squeezed into a corner of St
Sulpice. The darkness is impenetrable beneath the vaulted roof.
Lost in its infinity, powerless against its might, multitudes of
tiny flames are flickering before the altars to the saints, all gen-
uflecting in the same direction when shadows pass them and
footsteps ring out coldly against the stone paving. Her ears are
full of such ecclesiastical footsteps, she has listened to so many
of them during the day, long able to distinguish the flat soles of
the priests from those of other people, the young from the old,
men from women.

She has no idea of the time. Vespers is over. Tall candles
were lighted at the altar, pushing back a little of the darkness,
modelling out of it rows of faces into warm, restless
chiaroscuro. The scent of fresh incense cut into the old, stag-
nant smell, murmuring in Latin alternated with thin, urgent
ringing of bells, the tiny, zealous silhouettes of the choirboys
moved up and down the altar steps, coming, going, genuflect-
ing. That must have been a long time ago.

He came in at some point, suddenly leaning over her in the
dimness, a fragment of vanishing daylight from a high window
falling on this tense face. She could see him only vaguely.
Nevertheless it struck her that his expression was similar to
that of the poor, a look of timid defiance, a slight twist to the
mouth when he spoke. He had knocked in vain at more than
one door. Nobody was at home, they were not even at the
Dôme. God knows where they all were. This one and that one
were said to have moved to a hotel, a hotel with central heating. Now he was going to try someone else. She would have to
be patient a little longer.

He had managed to find a franc somewhere or other. They spent it on hot milk at a bar nearby, and chestnuts. It tasted good for a moment or two, but roused their hunger. And it was really uncomfortable to have to move about, stiff and sore as she was from sitting so long. She looked forward to curling up inside the church again.

He refused to give it up and stay with her. 'Hasn't it occurred to you that we haven't a roof over our heads tonight?' he said. 'We can't go home until we have something to build a fire with.'

Oh yes, it had occurred to her all right.

'And on Christmas Eve, too.'

'We must stop thinking about Christmas Eve. We're not children.' She swallowed something childish that was trying to surface through her throat in spite of everything.

'Go and sit down again inside.'

She cried a little as she watched him disappear into the dusk and the crowds, one of the many hurrying along to beg for the simplest necessities. It seemed to her that he had a new way of walking, a poor man's walk, his shoulders hunched up and his hands plunged deep into his pockets. He kept close to the walls of houses, walking in the way the homeless and penniless walk. She was so tired that she did not notice anything clearly any more, but this cut her to the heart. Surely we're not really poor? she thought.

She returned to the drowsy, incense-laden air of the church.

It is getting crowded, people are shuffling about, whispering, coughing. The cold light from a couple of electric lamps suddenly falls over the nave, chairs are being arranged; one or two old ladies, who have arrived in good time for midnight mass, find their places and doze. Working-class women arrive, burdened with little children clinging to their skirts or in their arms. They bring a gust of winter with them in their clothes. The smell of poverty mingles with the air of the church.

She stopped thinking long ago. But a sequence of isolated images is floating in a disorganized way through her brain, sometimes joining up into painfully clear visions: a bed ready for the night with flickering flames from a fire, a steaming soup-tureen, a hot bath.

The naïve authors of the telegram appear as distant and unreal as characters in a sentimental story; a little circle of people round a Christmas tree, the gleam of the candles reflected in their kind, ingenuous eyes. She can imagine them asking one another the perennial question, 'Shouldn't Gustav go in for something else? This painting . . .? He doesn't sell any of it, does he?'

Supposing they came and asked her? Would she answer as she usually did, would she . . .?

. . . Nobody cares about them, nobody notices them. They are just two pieces of flotsam, floating on a boundless darkness that is drawing them into the whirlpool and will suck them under . . .

Far away on the beach are crowds of people. She catches sight of a childhood friend, an uncle, the sexton's wife at the place in the country where she used to stay as a child, the pharmacist over in the Rue des Plantes. All of them are drag-ging and carrying things, all of them are busy, all of them have somewhere to go. She calls to the pharmacist with all her might, 'We're drowning, we're drowning.' He hesitates. But she is only a piece of flotsam, and he goes away again . . .

. . . goes in through the school gate in the village at home. It leads to heaven. That's where they're all going.

. . . the assembly hall in the school at home, the vault of heaven bathed in light, scents and sounds streaming through it. They come from everywhere and nowhere. The air itself is ringing and singing, bringing light and warmth with it, for no source of light is visible . . .

. . . a garden . . . the garden at home . . . it's spring, she is picking flowers.

Suddenly she is sitting bolt upright and realizes that she has been asleep and dreaming. But the dream accompanies her into reality. Squeezed among crowds of people standing and sitting around her, she can still hear the air ringing and singing. The splendour of midnight mass is filling the church.

She looks round in confusion and finds a back she recog-nizes, a back in a raincoat and the fact that goes with it. She can see it in half-profile, tilted upwards. All bitterness seems to have been smoothed away from it. It is young, calm, lost in untroubled listening, beautiful. It is like a reunion with the happiness they both shared before everything became so con-tentious and difficult. She stares at it in amazement. What is real, this, or the cold and darkness outside?

She feels strengthened and renewed. It was not heaven, but it was a moment's rest from the grimness of life. Someone is nudging her: a young working wife whispers, 'It helps to take a little nap now and again.'

As if prompted she looks down into her lap, at her hands. And now the dream continues, now she is dreaming that she is dreaming. Her hands are lying there and they are her hands, but a bunch of violets has been put into them. She stares at them for a while, then lifts them to her face. They *are* real, smelling at first only of moss and a damp cellar. And then of spring and of life.

He has managed a loan after all. And he is completely untroubled again. And he has brought violets for her because it is Christmas. That was kind of him.

She tugs at his coat. 'Thank you.'

He smiles down at her. 'Are you awake? Did you know you'd fallen asleep? You look like a different person. The mass has just begun.'

'How much did you get?'

He whispers the figure. He puts his finger to his lips. They must be quiet for the sake of all those sitting around them. With a triumphant expression he turns his back to her.

After a while she tugs at his coat a second time. She cannot stop worrying: 'We can never pay it back.'

'Pay it back? I've had a sale, silly-billy. At home in Haugesund. Met a fellow who's been looking for me all day. Gave me some of it in advance – hush . . .'

Dumbly she leans back against the wall. After a while she starts singing: a hymn about Christmas and redemption.

It was no fortune. Three hundred kroner, if the truth must be told. But it meant food, warmth, a night in a hotel, at least one. Firewood, payment of the rent, a reprieve from poverty and ruin, new possibilities, new hopes . . .

It is midnight. Crushed and pressed by the throng they are gradually pushed towards the exit, while the Christmas carols echo beneath the vaults and the bells in the tower reverberate through the roar of the organ.

The air streaming to meet them from outside is different from before. It is snowing. Thickly and softly and generously. There will be a thaw. The air tastes of childhood; it tastes of Norway.

The square is white. The fountain with its three enormous basins, each one inside the other, is etched in thick, fuzzy contours. Each black tree carries, and is united with, a white one. But the wheel-tracks in the street are already grey and wet. Here and there among the houses in the background the mist parts and light falls through it. The gleam from the arc lamps falls on to the square in large circles, giving it the air of a stage on which symbolic events are to be played out.

'What a motif!' Immediately he frames it all with his hands, moving them here and there to get the composition right, squinting through his eyes with his head on one side. 'What a motif! But I know someone who's going to have hot onion soup. And maybe turkey. And maybe wine. I know someone who's going to sleep at a hotel tonight and maybe tomorrow night. And pay the grocery bill and the café bill and the rent and the paint shop and buy firewood and tea and sole her shoes and . . . come along.'

They walk away quickly, arm in arm. Their bodies are springy and supple because they have money in their pockets and fresh credit. Because they can see the road ahead for just a little way.

'The still life,' he says. 'Damn me if I don't set up that still life again. I saw a jug exactly like it in Montparnasse yesterday.'

She feels like a traitor because just for an instant she permitted herself the thought that perhaps Gustav ought to go in for something else.

Edith Nesbit
(1858–1924)

Born in London, but educated in a French convent, Edith Nesbit began her literary career by writing poetry, and became acquainted with the Rossettis and their circle. She is best known as a writer of children's books, including *The Story of the Treasure Seekers* (1899) and *The Railway Children* (1906), but she also wrote novels and ghost stories. A woman of great personal and physical charm, she was one of the founding members of the Fabian Society. Her first husband, writer Hubert Bland, was an incurable philanderer, and she accepted his illegitimate offspring into their household. After the death of Bland, she married the engineer Thomas Tucker. The poem here, wistful and whimsical, is called 'A Clerk's Christmas Dream'.

The office hours were ended
A little while ago,
And friendly and unfriended
Alike must homeward go.
Long since the noontide's high light
Died on the office skylight,
And dreary winter twilight
Was lost in gas-lit glow.

I tread the pavement crowded
With busy city men,
Whose souls dark veils have shrouded,
Woven by ink and pen.
Were but the veils once lifted,
The money-mist back-drifted,
What visions changed and shifted
Would rise before them then!

For me, my fancy ranges
O'er silent hill and plain;
The noisy pavement changes
Into a country lane,
Where crushed dead leaves are lying,
And day and year are dying,
And winter winds are sighing
Their desolate refrain.

Past ghostly elms and beeches,
Past hedgerows gaunt and bare,
My yearning heart outreaches
Through frosty Christmas air
To her, to her, my treasure,
My only prize and pleasure,
Belovèd beyond measure,
And good beyond compare.

I thread the lanes and meadows,
I know each inch of way;
'Twas here we saw our shadows
Cast by the moon of May.
With red, wet eyes that smarted,
Here at the church we parted,
Each almost broken-hearted,
The night I went away.

About her gate the roses
No more are sweet and red,
And all the snow discloses
Are rose-thorns brown and dead;
But through her window gleaming
Her lamp's warm glow is streaming –
The star of all my dreaming,
Which here my steps has led.

Haste through the gate – go faster,
O feet, if that may be,
And bear your eager master
To where she waits for me;
And haste, O longed-for hour,
Of all my life the flower,
When in her winter bower
Mine eyes my rose shall see!

Love, I am here – O vision,
Dead e'er it gained its crown!
But that is Fate's derision,
And this is Camden Town;
And dreams of love's creating
Fly at my latch-key's grating,
And Christmas bills are waiting –
Good-evening, Mrs Brown.

Phoebe Cary
(1824–71)

Phoebe Cary was born on her father's farm near Cincinnati. Like her older sister, Alice, she was a poet, and their collected works, *The Poems of Alice and Phoebe Cary*, were published in 1849. Phoebe's literary output was smaller than her sister's, but it has been said that she wrote with greater wit and feeling. Her books include *Poems and Parodies* (1854) and *Poems of Faith, Hope and Love* (1858). The sisters were devoted to one another and died within months of each other in 1871.

'The Wife's Christmas' is a pathetic tale of domestic loneliness, all the more touching for its lack of pretension.

How can you speak to me so, Charlie!
It isn't kind, nor right;
You wouldn't have talked a year ago,
As you have done to-night.

You are sorry to see me sit and cry,
Like a baby vexed, you say;
When you didn't know I wanted a gift,
Nor think about the day!

But I'm not like a baby, Charlie,
Crying for something fine;
Only a loving woman pained,
Could shed such tears as mine.

For every Christmas time till now –
And that is why I grieve –
It was you that wanted to give, Charlie,
More than I to receive.

And all I ever had from you
I have carefully laid aside;
From the first June rose you pulled for me,
To the veil I wore as a bride.

And I wouldn't have cared to-night, Charlie,
How poor the gift or small;
If you only had brought me something to show
That you thought of me at all.

The merest trifle of any kind,
That I could keep or wear;
A flimsy bit of lace for my neck,
Or a ribbon for my hair.

Some pretty story of lovers true,
Or a book of pleasant rhyme;
A flower, or a holly branch, to mark
The blessèd Christmas time.

But to be forgotten, Charlie!
'Tis that that brings the tear;
And just to think, that I haven't been
Your wife but a single year!

Clare Boylan
(1948–)

Clare Boylan was born and brought up in Dublin. She worked as a journalist from 1966 to 1981, after which she became a radio and television broadcaster. Her debut novel, *Holy Pictures* (1983), was set in Dublin in the 1920s and tells the story of two sisters, Nan and Mary Cantwell, who are in the process of shedding their childhood. It met with enormous acclaim in Europe as well as the United States. Boylan's novels often reveal a fascination with childhood and the loss of innocence. Her style, witty and rich in unusual imagery, is much praised. Clare Boylan has also edited *The Agony and the Ego, the Art and Strategy of Fiction Writing Explored* (1993) and *The Literary Companion to Cats* (1994). Her other titles include *A Nail in the Head* (1983), *Last Resorts* (1984), *Concerning Virgins* (1990), *That Bad Woman* (1995) and *Room for a Single Lady* (1997).

This story, 'The Alternative Christmas', comes from *Another Family Christmas* (1997).

On the previous Christmas Maeve had saved for three months to buy her husband a new set of golf clubs and he had surprised her with a set of padded coat hangers. She had upset Juliet, her daughter, by innocently opening the locket her boyfriend had given her and discovering the tissue-wrapped Ecstasy tablet inside. Pete, the baby, had wanted a new laptop computer costing fifteen hundred pounds and when she protested that she couldn't afford it he confessed that he couldn't abide her.

If she opened a magazine at this time of year, it was full of magical pictures of forests blooming in drawing rooms, glass icicles hanging from trees glowing with tiny tasteful lights. There were drapes of ivy and golden bows on the mantelpieces, cards nestling amid dangerous but glamorous chandeliers. Table settings were bacchanal with pagodas of hothouse fruits, decanters of ruby wine, nuts and glacéed chestnuts; or else palely tasteful with napkins twisted into winged angels and cascades of scented freesias and Christmas roses. There were little rosy children with tumbling curls and party dresses and, presiding over all of this, a calm, beautiful woman dressed in some unlikely garment of tartan grosgrain.

Maeve wondered about the woman, whose fingers must have been sticky for months on end from glacéing *marrons* and sieving cranberries and mixing stuffing and making mince and crimping filo pastry and macerating clementines and rolling home-made *petits fours* in cocoa powder. What was in it for her? What was in it for any woman? Women, who rarely earned any money, suddenly became a conduit for cash, expected to fund their children's urgent need for new outfits, to find gifts for every member of their husband's family as well as buying all the costly groceries. Everyone else was pampered and indulged but women were supposed to be overwhelmed if someone flung them a potted plant, a tin of talc, a set of matching tea towels.

This Christmas, something inside her had snapped. She felt completely incapable of grappling with one more naked turkey, of shopping for Brian's innumerable aunts. She must be coming down with something. It was only two days to Christmas and she lay in bed, wanly doodling with a shopping list while glancing through the newspaper. She was reading the small adds, as women do when they are despondent, just as women in love read their horoscopes. She was drifting off when a small notice caught her eye.

'ALTERNATIVE CHRISTMAS. Are you a hard-pressed housewife, sick of the drudgery of the festive season? There's still time for a really different, self-indulgent Christmas. No cost, no work, no catch. Call Sandra at . . .' And it listed a city centre number.

She had once tried an alternative Christmas, which suggested a dinner of roasted venison and chocolate mousse. The venison resembled, in taste and texture, a log of pine. Her mousse came out of the fridge looking like Grimpen Mire. She put a cherry on the top and it sank without trace. Its cries were horrible. She did not really believe that there was any alternative to Christmas – no alternative and no escape either – but she phoned Sandra and went into town.

She was surprised she had not noticed the office before. It

was one of those little side doors in Duke Street. *Alternative Christmas Inc.* it said in gold letters, and underneath, in smaller print, 'Women only.'

'So,' Maeve asked Sandra, 'what is the alternative?'

'What would you like?' Sandra was tall and glamorous in a tight red dress.

Maeve laughed. 'I'd like to stay in bed all day drinking champagne.'

Sandra wrote this down. 'Alone?'

Maeve shrugged. She had heard about women without families who went off to Venice for Christmas or stayed in bed with a lover.

'You'd like a lover?' Sandra pressed helpfully.

'Well, I hadn't thought . . .' she lied.

'What kind of lover?' Sandra persisted.

Maeve was stumped. 'I'm afraid I don't know anything about lovers.'

'How about the world's most perfect lover?'

Maeve laughed. 'Look, this is a joke, isn't it?'

Sandra put her hands on her hips. 'Why do women always think it's a joke when anyone tries to do something nice for them?'

'I'm a married woman,' Maeve protested.

'You've heard of indulgences, haven't you? Penances you perform to knock some time off your term in purgatory. Well, when a woman has put in a sufficient number of Christmases, she has earned an indulgence. That's all this is. It's an indulgence.'

'Who are you?' Maeve asked.

'My full name is Sandra Claus. I'm the patron saint of unap-
preciated married women. Of course, I'm not an official saint.
I have some radical ideas, but I have performed miracles.'

'How come no one's ever heard of you?'

'Oh, lots of women know about me,' Sandra winked.
'Naturally they don't go around talking about it. They wouldn't
want their families to know.'

'Which reminds me,' Maeve said, 'while I'm off gallivanting
with this, this . . . gigolo . . . who's going to look after my
family?'

Sandra poured them each a glass of wine. 'They could look
after themselves. But I can see that shocks you. No, what we do
is we send in a look-alike to do all the work. We have a
humanatronics factory that turns out perfect replicas of our
clients. Anyone could do all that crap that women do at
Christmas. No one will know the difference. Now, look hard-
pressed. I just have to take some Polaroids for our crafts people.'

The days coming up to Christmas passed in the usual
fraught fashion. On Christmas Eve she went to bed exhausted.
When she woke next morning she had forgotten all about her
curious encounter. She lay there, reluctant to move, then sat up
with a start. What was that smell? Good heavens, it was coffee.
Beside her on the bed was a tray set with fragrant coffee, but-
tery croissants, home-made jam. As the taste of the coffee woke
her up she looked around. The whole room had changed. It
wasn't her bedroom at all. She was in a baroque chamber, pink
and gilt with vast mirrors and little silk-covered lamps. Where
the hell was she? There was a knock on the door. 'Brian?' she
said.

He sprang through the door bearing a bottle of champagne and two glasses. 'Not Brian, my little passion-flower. Bernardo!'

He was very good-looking but there was rather a lot of him and he wasn't, frankly, overdressed. He was wearing a small towel which appeared to be working its way loose. He pranced over to the bed, set down the champagne and leaned forward to kiss her. He was a nice kisser. When he sprang into bed, Maeve had the sudden, depressing thought that she should have asked Sandra for a new figure. How on earth could she face Bernardo with stretch marks and Sloggi underwear? He didn't seem to mind. 'To our day of bliss. Are you content, my little sugar pumpkin?'

Well, I'm not miserable, she thought. I'm not worn-out, harassed, picked-on. His moustaches tickled her as he kissed her again.

'What shall we do first? I know! How about some presents?' From beside the bed he produced three gift-wrapped boxes. In between sips of champagne she undid the bows. There was a wonderful silk dressing-gown which she had gazed at in the window of Susan Hunter, a perfect little black dress by Jean Muir which she had fingered wistfully in Brown Thomas and a set of La Perla underwear in rose-coloured silk from Fogal. They were the kind of clothes she always thought were much too good for her, and yet she had known she would look well in them. She went into the bathroom, sprayed herself with perfume and put on the silk underwear. Now I'm content, she thought.

'I'm afraid I've got nothing for you,' she apologised to Bernardo. 'Oh, yes you have, my precious little potpourri,'

he said huskily. 'You have everything I could possibly desire.'
She was getting rather fond of him. For one thing, he seemed
terribly easy to please. She had a momentary pang of conscience as she got back into bed but then she thought, 'Oh,
well, they did warn that this sort of thing would happen if the
divorce referendum went through. I suppose there's no going
back now.'

'What would you like?' He swept her into his arms.

'I'm not fussy, really.'

Be rebuked her gently. 'Do not insult the world's greatest
lover by acting as if you were dining in a factory canteen. It is
within my power to give you undreamed-of pleasure.'

'Fire away.' She closed her eyes.

'You have to say what you want.' He began to look a tiny bit
peevish.

'I'm sorry, Bernardo,' she said. 'I don't know what I want. I'm
a married woman.'

He looked decidedly disgruntled now. 'Women always com-
plain that they are treated unfairly, but how can anyone make
them happy when they refuse to express their desires? Haven't
you ever had any fantasies?'

She agreed that she had. She had a fantasy about being in
bed with the kind of man who would massage her shoulders
when she was tired, someone she could have a laugh with
under the blankets.

Bernardo's moustaches quivered. 'A laugh? You want to
laugh at the world's greatest lover?'

'I won't laugh.' She sighed.

'You don't appreciate me,' he sniffed. 'That's the trouble with women today. They demand sexual equality, but they are still coy and prudish. I, a sexual athlete of Olympic standards, am expected to conduct a solo performance while you lie there like an . . . an . . . aerobics mat.'

Maeve suppressed a sigh. She looked longingly at the champagne. 'Maybe you could suggest a few things.'

'How about cocoa, carol singing, the Christmas panto on telly?' he said huffily.

Maeve suddenly thought they suddenly didn't sound too bad.

'I have given over my entire life to the service of women,' Bernardo complained. 'I have made love to them, flattered them, fulfilled them, I have liberated their sexuality. Do you think they are grateful? Not at all. What do they all say? Do you love me, Bernardo?' Great lovers are wasted on women. All they really want is to be reassured.'

'Maybe you ought to try a man.' Maeve gave vent to irony.

He looked at her in astonishment. 'That is an extraordinary thing to say.'

'I didn't mean anything,' she said quickly.

'No, no! It's just that I was beginning to think the same thing myself. The only problem is, even in this day and age one still has doubts.' As Bernardo began to confide his doubts, Maeve snuggled down. After a while she found that she need no longer listen, but merely offer occasional soothing responses. 'Poor Bernardo,' she murmured sleepily.

'Who's Bernardo?' Juliet was peering down at her.

Maeve sat bolt upright. She stared at the other side of the bed.

'Mum, are you all right?' Juliet said. 'Why are you goggling at the duvet?'

'Is this my bedroom?' She peered cautiously around. There was her own faded rose wallpaper, the drooping curtains that she kept meaning to replace.

'I must have fallen asleep while I was making out the shopping list. What day is it?'

'It's Saturday. It's two days to Christmas and there's nothing done! Mum, stop raving. I need fifty quid.'

'You mean, it was all a dream?' Maeve said.

'What was all a dream?' Juliet said irritably. 'I have to go out. I need the money now, Mum.'

Maeve found she could barely remember the dream, except for one phrase which stuck vividly in her mind. 'Get my bag.'

'Oh, thanks, Mum!'

Maeve handed her the shopping list. 'You can have the fifty pounds – as soon as you've done all the shopping.'

Juliet scanned the list and let out a howl. 'That's not fair! It's all the groceries and all the presents, including Dad's countless lousy relations. It'll take the whole day. And how am I supposed to drag all this home?'

'How do you suppose I dragged it all home for the last twenty years?' Maeve asked. 'Get Pete to help you.'

'No, Mum!' Juliet stood her ground.

'No money!' Maeve explored her own.

After Juliet had stamped out with the shopping basket, Maeve made some phone calls. The last of these was to her husband. 'Brian, dear, have you got my presents yet?'

'Brian's response was terse. 'I'm rather busy. I'll pick up something for you at lunch-time.'

'I know you're busy,' she said, 'so I decided to save you some trouble. Remember those lovely hangers you bought me last year! Well, this year I want something to hang on them.' She described the Jean Muir at Brown Thomas, the dressing-gown from Susan Hunter, the rose-coloured lingerie.

'You don't expect me to go charging through women's dress shops the day before Christmas Eve?' Brian scoffed.

'Of course not, sweetie,' she soothed. 'I've already phoned the shops and given them my size and your credit card number. The presents will be wrapped and sent around to your office.'

As she lay in her bath with a bottle of champagne pilfered from Brian's cellar she thought about the dream and, in particular, the phrase of Bernardo's.

'You have to say what you want.' She drank a toast. 'To Bernardo, my liberator.' The champagne was delicious so she drank another toast. 'To Sandra Claus!' And she began to look forward to a really different, self-indulgent Christmas.

Stephanie June Sorrell
(1956–)

Stephanie Sorrell was born in Barnet, north London. A free-lance writer for some 20 years, she has published romances for the commercial market and has written poetry and articles on alternative health and astrology. For the last seven years she has worked as editor for *New Vision*, a bi-monthly, spiritually ori-entated magazine. Her most recent book is *Trusting the Process*. Her work often focuses on nature, cats and travelling and is fre-quently published in anthologies. 'The Christmas Rose' is published here for the first time.

All summer she dreamed
in her underground ice palace.
As wave upon wave of golden fire
consumed the earth.

She dreamed of her knight riding from Antarctica.
Saw his ice sculpted cheekbones and eyes
of sapphire flame that would waken her from sleep.
A tear of longing formed a white icicle on her frosted
    lash
as she waited.

She dreamed of his arrival,
Heard the sound of his approaching steed
as the sparks leapt hungrily beneath the galloping
    hooves.
He would waken her, bring her to life.

She dreamed, until suddenly he was bending over her,
his lips finding the pink petals of her own.
Until half smiling, half dreaming,
she opened her eyes.

Blushing, she stretched and pressed upwards
from her ice palace to meet his kiss.
She awoke, gasping from the heat of his passion,
moisture collecting in dewdrops on her taut
petals on the first day of her blooming upon
the December earth.

Amy Lowell
(1874–1925)

Amy Lowell was born into a wealthy family in Brookline, Massachusetts. She was educated privately and travelled extensively in Europe with her family. She started writing poetry around 1902. In 1913 she met Ezra Pound and became one of the 'Imagist poets', a group which he co-founded. Later she began to write 'polyphonic prose', a kind of rhythmic prose similar to free verse, her best known piece being 'Patterns'. She also wrote *vers libre*, which she called 'unrhymed cadence'. Lowell was an eccentric figure who smoked cigars and allegedly slept on sixteen pillows, but her biography of John Keats, which was published in the year of her death from a cerebral haemorrhage, was a work of meticulous scholarship. Her poem 'A New Year's Card', is from *Ballads for Sale*.

Everyone has his fancies, I suppose,
And to-night I should like to walk round a towered
   city
Blowing a blue silver trumpet.
Then, when all the people had run out
To see me circling the walls
Playing on a blue trumpet,
I would stop and sing them a song all about your
   loveliness.
I would make it of the flicker of the air and the sweep
   of the sun,
And when I had finished, they would see you sitting
   on a cloud
And know how far you surpassed others in
   everything.
But there is no towered city,
And I have no blue trumpet,
And those who meet you seem to feel about you
   much as I do without the aid of these accessories,
Which proves how very useless a thing a poet is, after
   all.

Acknowledgements

Virago gratefully acknowledges the following for permission to reprint copyright material.

'Letter from Egypt' by Moira Andrew, copyright © Moira Andrew, 1988. First published in *A Christmas Stocking*, edited by Wes Magee, Cassell 1988.

Curiouser and Curiouser by Sue Arnold, published by Constable and Company Ltd. Copyright © Sue Arnold, 1985. Reprinted by permission of Constable & Robinson.

The Christmas Tree by Isabel Bolton, first published by Charles Scribner's Sons 1949. Copyright © Isabel Bolton, 1949, renewed 1997 by James Miller. Reprinted by permission of Russell & Volkening, Inc., as agents for the author's estate.

'The Alternative Christmas' from *Another Family Christmas* by Clare Boylan, published by Poolbeg Press Ltd. Copyright © Clare Boylan, 1997. Reprinted by permission of Rogers, Coleridge & White.

Testament of Youth by Vera Brittain, published by Victor

'No Room at the Inn' by Edna Ferber, first published in 1939 by Crowell-Collier Publishing Co. Reprinted by permission of Julie Gilbert.

Memoirs of a Fir Tree, The Life of Elsa Tannenbaum by Rachel Ferguson, published by Nicholson & Watson in 1946. Copyright © Rachel Ferguson, 1946. Reprinted by permission of Campbell, Thomson & McLaughlin Ltd.

A Child in the Forest by Winifred Foley, published 2001 by Doug McLean. First published by BBC Publications in 1974. Copyright © Winifred Foley, 1974, 2001.

'Christmas at Cold Comfort Farm' from *Christmas at Cold Comfort Farm and Other Stories* by Stella Gibbons, copyright © Stella Gibbons, 1940. Reprinted by permission of Curtis Brown Ltd., London.

Towers in the Mist by Elizabeth Goudge, published by Gerald Duckworth & Co Ltd. Reprinted by permission of David Higham Associates Ltd.

'Papoo Yaya' by Laurie Graham reprinted by permission of the author. Copyright © Laurie Graham 2002.

'The Christmas Present' by Kathleen Hersom, copyright © Kathleen Hersom, 1986. First published in *The Oxford Book of Christmas Stories*, edited by Dennis Pepper, published by Oxford University Press. Reprinted by permission of the publishers.

Peters, Fraser and Dunlop on behalf of the Estate of Nancy Mitford.

'Poem for Christmas Day' from *A Blue Harvester Mug* by Kathleen Norcross, published by the Birmingham and Midland Institute. Copyright © Kathleen Norcross, 1990. Reprinted by permission of the author.

The Homesick Garden by Kate Cruise O'Brien, published by Poolbeg Press Ltd. Copyright © Kate Cruise O'Brien, 1991.

The Silken Thread, Stories and Sketches by Cora Sandel, translated from the Norwegian and with an introduction by Elizabeth Rokkan, published by Peter Owen Publishers. Copyright © Cora Sandel and Peter Owen Ltd. 1986, English translation copyright © Elizabeth Rokkan and Peter Owen Ltd, 1986.

Sassafrass, Cypress and Indigo by Ntozake Shange, published by Methuen. Copyright © Ntozake Shange, 1982. Reprinted by permission of A. M. Heath & Co. Ltd.

Selected Letters of Edith Sitwell, edited by Richard Greene, published by Virago Press. Copyright © E.T.S. Sitwell and Richard Greene, 1997, 1998. Reprinted by permission of David Higham Associates Ltd.

'The Christmas Rose' by Stephanie June Sorrell. Copyright © Stephanie June Sorrell, 2002. Reprinted by permission of the author.